RELATIONSHIP REVIVAL

RELATIONSHIP REVIVAL

8 PILLARS OF A STRONG, CONNECTED & FULFILLING RELATIONSHIP

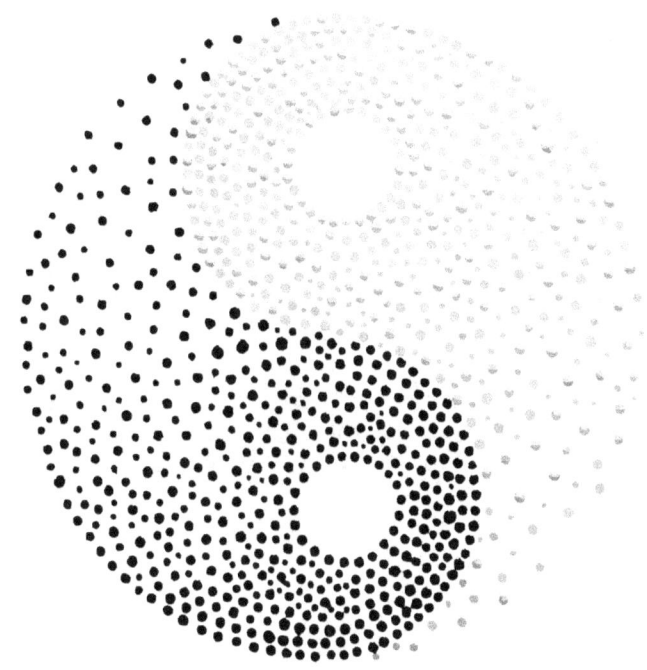

CHERYL PAIGE

Relationship Revival
Copyright © 2018 by Cheryl Paige

All rights reserved. No part of this book may be reproduced in any part by any means—graphic, electronic, or mechanical—without the prior written permission of the publisher, except by a reviewer, who may use brief excerpts in a review.

The author of this book does not dispense medical advice or prescribe the use of any technique, either directly or indirectly, as a form of treatment for physical, emotional, or medical problems, without the advice of a physician. The author's intent is only to offer information of a general nature to help you in your quest for emotional, physical, and spiritual well-being. In the event you use any of the information in this book, the author and the publisher assume no responsibility for your actions.

Cover Design by Vanessa Ooms
Edited by Shirarose Wilensky
Book Design by Maureen Cutajar
Author Photo by Ashly Narula Photography

Print ISBN: 978-1-7753834-0-6
E-book ISBN: 978-1-7753834-1-3

The intent of the author is to offer general information. The use of the information provided in this book is a personal choice. The author and publisher assumes no responsibility.

To my beloved, Jaye,
for your unconditional love, support and willingness
to share our journey. I love you xoxo

CONTENTS

PROLOGUE 1

INTRODUCTION: The Polarity of Love. 5

PILLAR 1: Make a Choice. 11

PILLAR 2: Clean up Your Side of the Street. 15

PILLAR 3: Design Your Ultimate Relationship Vision. 45

PILLAR 4: Learn Loving & Effective Communication. 61

PILLAR 5: Create Your Emotional Connection. 85

PILLAR 6: Ignite Your Sexual Connection 103

PILLAR 7: Let Go of the Past. 131

PILLAR 8: Get on the Same Team 153

CONCLUSION. 181

EPILOGUE. 183

ACKNOWLEDGEMENTS & GRATITUDE. 185

PROLOGUE

On a crisp, windy fall day, the coloured leaves floated from the trees as we looked into each other's eyes. My veil flowed with the wind and Jaye's eyes twinkled with his signature smirk. We each held a vase full of sand: mine white and his black. With all of our friends and family smiling and watching, we slowly poured the two colours of sand into a larger vase. This symbolized the importance of us as individuals within the marriage and the coming together of our two lives. The bottom of the larger vase was lined with a layer of neutral-coloured river rocks that grounded the marriage and formed the foundation we would build upon—the life experiences we had each had before we married and those we would have together in the future. We smiled at each other with great love in anticipation of the journey we were embarking on, with little idea of how complicated and difficult it would be to blend together two lives.

I grew up watching fairy tales, not only in the movies but also in real life. My grandparents were married for sixty-two years, and they danced at our wedding, looking into each other's eyes with the same love and adoration they always had. My parents' thirty-third wedding anniversary was the day before we got married. They all made marriage look so easy.

I was bred to be a romantic, but our marriage hasn't turned out to be the fairy tale I had imagined. Easy like my grandparents and parents made it seem? No. Our marriage has taken us to places we never imagined in our wildest dreams. It's made us face parts of ourselves we didn't even know existed. Our relationship has been the biggest and most challenging classroom of both our lives. At times, we have felt so broken and defeated that we couldn't fathom how to begin to come together again. The gridlock of those times left us exhausted and depleted. A fairy tale? Hell, no—at times it felt more like a nightmare.

But through these trials, we have learned that marriage is a journey. It's a process of becoming, of learning, of growing and of evolving. A place where our souls see each other and honour each other. A place where we *work* extremely hard at times to remember that we have joined our lives together, but that we are individuals first with our own unique dreams, beliefs and opinions. We have come to understand that we are not required to agree on everything, and that disagreeing doesn't mean the other person is wrong.

Our marriage is a dance where we sometimes stumble. We yearn for more. We struggle to stay connected. We make room for each other to continue to grow, to continue to emerge, to continue to change and evolve. And we hold space for the other person to spread their wings and fly in the direction that is right for them. Sometimes it's hard. Sometimes it's *really damn hard*, but we dance. It's a dance where each of us leads at different times. Sometimes we slow dance; sometimes we Latin dance with arms flying. Sometimes we trip each other. Other times we glide across the dance floor like we are one. What we have discovered, though, is we are not one. We are two.

Prologue

Two souls that have come together in this physical world as partners in life. And because we are in an intimate relationship and see each other every single day, we see the best of each other—and the worst.

As the years passed, the sand that we poured into the vase on our wedding day has became more than symbolic. We have realized that the individuals the black sand and the white sand represented would have to not only combine but also honour each other's difference. It got real very quickly. Where one was strong, the other was weak. Where one was wounded, the other was healed. Where one was shut down, the other was emotional. Where one was soft, the other was hard. Where one yelled, the other stayed silent. Where one cried, the other stayed strong.

My relationship with Jaye has proven to be one of my greatest teachers on my journey of self-discovery. It pushes me constantly to look within. To evaluate what's inside me. Who I am. What I believe. Where I am hurt. Where there are scars. It challenges me constantly to expand, to emerge, more and more. I used to buck against this. Feel hurt and frustrated by it. Now, those times of gridlock have subsided because we know now that this is what marriage is. It's our journey. It's our process. It brings us many lessons to learn from. It pushes us to grow, to evolve, to reflect, to be compassionate, to be empathetic, to love, to honour and to support. So, now we embrace it.

We still have nightmare moments, but our outlook has changed. Although we don't know what life will throw at us next, we know now that we can handle it. We've handled so much and it's only made us stronger. We are in this together. Our foundation is strong. We honour and support each other. We dance together, still pushing and pulling lots of the time, but now also realizing that the push and the pull *is* the dance. It's the marriage, and we are in it together.

INTRODUCTION

The Polarity of Love

"People think a soul mate is your perfect fit, and that's what everyone wants. But a true soul mate is a mirror, the person who shows you everything that is holding you back, the person who brings you to your own attention so you can change your life. A true soul mate is probably the most important person you'll ever meet, because they tear down your walls and smack you awake."
—Elizabeth Gilbert

Our relationships, especially those with our beloveds, are where some of our greatest growth takes place. Within relationships we will experience a great polarity of unbelievable bliss, love and joy—and shattering heartbreak, pain and sadness. To allow ourselves to love is to put ourselves into this world of polarity. If we close ourselves off from experiencing love because we're trying to protect ourselves from the pain that could occur, then we miss out on the bliss and joy that we could experience. It's a double-edged sword. At times, our relationships are the hardest things to be in, and at other times, they are the most amazing things to be a part of.

Our relationships are meant to have ups and downs. They are moving, dynamic entities with two human beings who possess two unique belief systems, sets of life experiences, and ways of seeing the world. When two people come together and try to mesh their different life stories, there are bound to be some fireworks. But these fireworks signify that our relationships have the ability to be our greatest teachers, should we choose to learn from them.

All of our relationships have different purposes. Though some are meant to last forever, the unrealistic story of riding off into the sunset and living happily ever after can lead us to feel like we are failing at our relationship, especially our intimate one with our beloved, when we have bumps and challenges. When it's not butterflies, batting eyelashes and happy, blissful excitement every day, then we feel like something must be wrong. Right? Wrong. There is no happily ever after. That's not reality. Reality is that relationships are hard at times. All relationships will challenge us and be full of difficult things to overcome. It's unrealistic to think that we shouldn't experience the polarity of love. We should, we will and we aren't alone. Everyone who is in a long-term relationship will experience these ups and downs. This ebb and flow is a natural part of an intimate relationship.

Other relationships enter our lives for a reason. They exist to teach us specific lessons, and then they end. Our job is to decipher which ones are lifetime relationships and which have run their course. This question has an ever-changing answer. As we change, the answer for each relationship may change. It is not set in stone.

We are here, on this earth, for this lifetime to learn, grow and evolve. Our lives are a big classroom and our relationships are our greatest teachers, delivering the most important lessons. Relationships and the dynamics that play out in them force us to face our deep wounds to heal what needs healing. To learn more and more about ourselves. To confront all the things that we thought we left behind. Our relationship with our beloved has a way of bringing all our "stuff" that lies right below the surface bubbling to the top. This is complicated and at times completely overwhelming.

Introduction

The kicker is that what's happening in our relationships is often a reflection of what's happening inside of us. A direct mirror for how we feel about ourselves. Relationships can feel complicated because they don't consist of just us. They also involve another being who has things happening inside of them. Their reflection is also being mirrored in the relationship. The mingling of these two stories and beings creates a relationship with great complexities.

Learning to manage ourselves within a relationship while all of our stuff, and our beloved's, is bubbling to the surface is a challenge. And in many cases it seems that it would be easier to just leave it all alone, or to leave the relationship. But the reality is this: where you go, there you are. We can't run from what's inside of us. It will continue to follow us into every relationship or circumstance in our life until we learn what we need to learn. There is no getting around it, so these are the questions we must ask ourselves:

- Am I going to learn this lesson in the relationship I'm in?
- Or have I learned all I can from this relationship?
- Am I going to move on to learn this lesson on my own?
- Or am I going to move on to another relationship to learn it there?

Only you can answer these questions for yourself. There are no right or wrong answers. There is only your inner knowing, which is always the right direction.

It is my deepest belief that as human beings our innate need to love and be loved is paramount to the quality of the life and relationships we experience. Several years ago, I found myself feeling really unhappy in my life. From the outside looking in, anyone would have guessed that I already had the life I dreamed of. I had a successful financial planning career; I was married with two beautiful, healthy kids; and I was surrounded by friends. Yet I was really unhappy, and

I couldn't figure out why. I was so disconnected from my authentic self that I didn't know what I wanted or needed or even felt.

So I embarked on a journey of self-discovery and soon realized that I had stopped listening to myself. And because I was so deeply disconnected from my authentic self, I was experiencing that disconnection within my intimate relationship with my beloved, Jaye, as well. We found ourselves in complete gridlock. In a cycle of blame and frustration. And it was so very painful.

Often in society we receive the message that if our relationship is not a fairy tale, then something is wrong. If we lose that feeling of butterflies in the belly, then it's time to reconsider. The shame around struggling in our relationships is real and fierce. Many of us aren't talking; we aren't sharing. We live in a world of perfect social media profiles depicting unrealistic lives. But this leads to us feeling isolated and alone and lost.

But when I started to open up about the struggles Jaye and I were facing in our relationship—with the pressures of working, raising a family, navigating situations with extended family and merging our two lives and two separate visions of a relationship into one—I quickly learned that many others, actually most others, had experienced similar struggles. And they too felt like they were the only ones.

I know now that we're not the only ones who have faced crisis in our relationship. Whose relationship has hit a state of gridlock, lost its connection, at one point or another. And as we don't exist on our own in this world, our relationships are often our greatest classroom. They teach us so very much about ourselves and about how we show up in the world.

In this book, we'll dive into our relationships with our beloveds and ourselves, and go on a journey of learning how to best use our relationships for our own personal growth and evolution. We'll discover how to revive our relationships using these 8 pillars:

Introduction

PILLAR 1: Make a Choice
PILLAR 2: Clean up Your Side of the Street
PILLAR 3: Design Your Ultimate Relationship Vision
PILLAR 4: Learn Loving & Effective Communication
PILLAR 5: Create Your Emotional Connection Plan
PILLAR 6: Ignite Your Sexual Connection
PILLAR 7: Let Go of the Past
PILLAR 8: Get on the Same Team

These pillars will form the stable foundation for a thriving relationship in which each person feels honoured and free. Each pillar is full of action steps that you can follow to revive your relationship. I encourage you to grab a journal that you'll use as you move through each pillar. To begin, do a quick read of the book, and then go back to the pillars that you identify as ones that require the most rebuilding in your relationship and begin to dig into the action steps. Please note that I provide many action steps, but it is not necessary to do every one of them. Pick the ones that resonate with you and begin by implementing a few. Know that it's normal to feel overwhelmed as you move through the process. Use this book like a reference guide. Pick it up over and over again as you move through the phases of your relationship as a guide and a support manual for building a strong, connected and fulfilling relationship.

Show love, kindness and compassion to yourself and your beloved as you embark on this beautiful journey of reviving your relationship. Remember to do what you can when you can, and know that whatever you can manage is enough. Think of yourself as a little kid learning to walk and treat yourself with gentleness. When a little one stands from the crawling position and takes their first wobbly step we cheer them on. When they inevitably fall down after that first step or two, we don't berate them and say, "What's wrong with you?!" We continue to encourage them as they master this new skill. Give yourself the same love, compassion, encouragement and praise as you learn and implement new ideas, skills and learnings throughout this book and in your life.

My mission now is to help and uplift others by sharing my learnings, frameworks and teachings to empower everyone with the tools and support they need to revive their relationships. What I share in this book is only my experience in my relationship with Jaye and where we are today in this moment. I am not naive enough to believe that things won't change. I don't pretend to know what the future holds for me or him, for us, or for anyone. I don't know where we will be in a year, in ten years or longer. We may find ourselves in a place where our relationship is no longer for our highest good, or we may find that we are continuing to grow and evolve within our relationship. Either way, I welcome what the future holds.

Let's dig in!

PILLAR 1

Make a Choice

"No matter what the situation, remind yourself, I have a choice."
—Deepak Chopra

I was catapulted onto this journey of self-discovery by the pain I felt in my relationship with my beloved, Jaye. I was on the brink of saying goodbye, but I first needed to try everything I could before I let go.

The first pillar of a strong, connected and fulfilling relationship is the decision to make a choice—are you in, or are you out. If you're on the brink of saying goodbye but first want to try everything you can before you let go, then my advice to you is this: while you are trying everything, get in it. Decide whether you are all in, for now, for this phase of trying everything. There's no chance of reviving your relationship if you have one foot out the door.

Put aside "the grass is greener on the other side" syndrome, for now. Change your frame of reference to "the grass is greener where we water it."

There will come a time when we hit rock bottom in our intimate relationship, when we are ripped wide open and become raw and vulnerable. When we look around and all we see is the rubble of a collapsed foundation—this is the time to rise and begin to rebuild with our beloved, or without. Check in with yourself before making this decision, as in many cases it can be life-altering. Are you trying to make this decision while the "grass" of your relationship is brown and dead because you've stopped watering it? Are you ready to begin to water it and see what happens? Or is the grass dead and never coming back to life?

It became clear to me that I wasn't ready to make the choice to leave until I did everything that I could to make the grass green and luscious again. I was blessed that Jaye was ready and willing to be all in with me at the same time. When we started this journey, our grass was brown and dead, but with two willing parties who were fully committed to watering their grass, the grass started to flourish again.

The ideas, concepts and teachings in this book are designed to help you revive your relationship. Sometimes that means staying in the one you're in, like I did, and building a stronger, more loving and honouring relationship. And sometimes that means acknowledging this relationship has fulfilled its purpose, has taught you the lessons it was meant to, and saying you're ready to close that chapter and begin a new one. Often this choice brings peace.

I'm not standing here on my soapbox saying that this is the way for everyone. I have respect, compassion and understanding for all relationship paths. I know that some relationships must come to an end. That sometimes all has been learned, and that chapter is closed. I know that many relationships experience things that cannot be overcome. I know that people grow apart, and sometimes they grow differently and no longer fit in the relationship as their new selves. I know that some people fight like hell to save their marriage before finally deciding to save themselves. It takes great courage to leave a relationship that is no longer serving you. This is a personal decision and no one else can make it for you. I support you in whatever decision you choose to make. I honour each relationship and each person's path.

I have a friend who recently ended her marriage and said to me, "I feel at peace." There is no greater thing than this. To feel peace is to feel alive. If you feel like you are slowly dying in your relationship and can't find peace, maybe the peace is outside of that relationship. I hope you follow your inner knowing and that peace comes to you.

A few years ago, I was having tea with another friend. She looked at me and said, "It doesn't matter what I do. I can't change it."

This wasn't the first time I'd heard words like this leave a friend's mouth, especially about an intimate relationship—and I could fully relate.

A few months earlier, I had been sitting in my counsellor's office and these words just flew out of my mouth: "I can understand how people have affairs." I wasn't having an affair, but my heart hurt. I felt empty. I was married, yet I felt completely and utterly alone. I felt like we were roommates who were emotionally and intimately disconnected, and we had found ourselves in a constant state of gridlock. I felt completely hopeless, like no matter what I did, the state of our marriage wasn't going to change. This deeply ingrained belief had left us both feeling powerless.

To become empowered, we have to embrace this truth: although we can't control what happens to us, we are the only people who can control how we react to what's happening. We have a choice. We can react by deciding that it doesn't matter what we do, which will lead us to feeling trapped, like we have no choice and that life is just happening to us. When we are in this state of mind, we'll experience bitterness, resentment and sadness. Or we can decide to be empowered by taking action and being in the state of mind that we are the captains of our own ships and we get to choose the direction we are going.

ACTION STEPS: MAKE A CHOICE

Our relationships can cause us great pain when we sit in limbo. Much of the unhappiness we experience is rooted in the belief that we have no control. Sitting there doing nothing, feeling stuck, not choosing a direction and not making a choice causes us pain and suffering. We will seek out a different path when the pain and suffering we are experiencing in our relationship becomes greater than the fear we have of asking for help, addressing issues and going down a road that we don't understand.

When we find ourselves paralyzed with indecision, and the pain and suffering are becoming more than we can bear—it is time to make a choice. In situations where we feel stuck and like we have no control we have three options:

1. Accept & Embrace the Relationship for What It Is
If we choose to accept and embrace the relationship, we no longer complain, commiserate with friends, bemoan our situation or find ways to rebel. We actively make the best of it, every day.

2. Change the Relationship
If we choose to stick with the relationship, we can change the situation by having a conversation with our beloved or implementing new ideas for a more satisfying relationship. We make the decision to stay in the relationship while working to change it for the better.

3. Leave the Relationship
If we choose to leave the relationship, we leave fully and move on. It's important to make this decision not out of frustration or desperation but after calm, measured consideration about what will make us happiest in the long term.

For all of these options *you* are in the driver's seat of your decision. It's time for *you* to decide which way *you* want to go. Building Pillar 1 means making a choice because living in indecision is causing you both great pain.

PILLAR 2

Clean up Your Side of the Street

"Until we have met the monsters in ourselves, we keep trying to slay them in the outer world. And we find that we cannot. For all darkness in the world stems from darkness in the heart. And it is there that we must do our work."

—MARIANNE WILLIAMSON

After you've built the first pillar of making a choice, the second pillar in reviving your relationship is cleaning up your side of the street. Only after we understand and nourish ourselves by taking care of our needs can we then be ready to dive deeply into the inner workings of our relationship with our beloved. First, we must steady our own self, because if we aren't happy in ourselves, if we aren't paying attention to our needs, development and growth, it's unlikely that we'll be able to experience happiness in our relationship. Our relationship can only be as happy as we are. It begins with us.

There are eight steps to cleaning up your side of the street:

1. Take Care of Yourself
2. Curb People-Pleasing
3. Become Aware of Your Self-Talk
4. Be Empowered
5. Turn Inwards
6. Connect with Your Inner Wisdom and Speak Your Truth
7. Reclaim Your Personal Power
8. Put Down Your Side of the Rope

STEP 1: TAKE CARE OF YOURSELF

The first step in cleaning up our side of the street is to take care of ourselves. We must realize that taking care of ourselves isn't selfish; it's necessary. We cannot take care of others if we are not filling our tank up first.

When we are not taking care of ourselves we seek fulfillment of our needs from external sources—often our relationship with our beloved. This puts extreme pressure on the relationship and leads to frustration when our impossible expectations are not met.

When we constantly put ourselves aside, we think we are being selfless, but in the end, we feel resentful, bitter and depleted. Often, we will find ourselves blaming these feelings on our relationship and searching for the solution in bettering and changing our relationship. This is not the answer. The real transformation begins with us.

- We begin to take care of ourselves by asking these important questions:
- Am I taking care of myself?
- What do I need?
- Am I meeting my own needs?
- When can I make time to take care of myself and meet my needs?

Life is busy so finding time for ourselves can be challenging. The following steps keep this in mind. The idea is not to add to your stress and things to do but rather to begin the process of learning how to take some time for you. Each suggestion is about becoming more aware. You can try all of the ideas or start with one.

Action Steps: Take Care of Yourself

In order to take care of others you need to be healthy. If you are unhappy, resentful, angry, exhausted and depleted, you will be unable to support others. Put your oxygen mask on first. The benefits will ripple out into your life to those who surround you—your family, and your beloved. Put your needs first and make sure that you take care of you—so that you can be fully present and able to take care of others.

1. Breathe for Five Minutes

This action step is all about reclaiming time for you to reconnect with yourself. When you first wake up in the morning and before you go to bed at night, take five minutes to sit quietly and take deep breaths, ideally through your mouth. I know it is awkward and totally unnatural—but so very effective!

While breathing, scan your body and listen to what it is telling you. You may notice your shoulders are tight, or your stomach is hurting. Maybe you have tingling in your body or feel warm or cold. Also pay attention to any emotions that come up and allow them to flow. This action step will start and end your day with a sense of clarity and calmness.

2. Do Something That Lights You Up Every Day

Whether it's chasing the kids around the back yard with water guns, going for a walk on the beach in your bare feet and feeling the sand between your toes or having a good ol' gab session full of belly laughs with your bestie, make it a priority to do something every single day that lights you up.

Step 2: Curb People-Pleasing

People are going to judge us no matter what we do, so we may as well do what is going to make us happy—from wearing what makes us feel good to preparing a five-course meal to meeting up with friends.

Action Steps: Curb People-Pleasing

Before you decide what you want to do, take a minute to consider why you want to do it. If the answer is because it makes you feel good and is true to you, then move forward with the decision. If it is because you are trying to make someone else happy, by putting what you want aside, then reconsider.

To curb our people-pleasing it is vital that we begin to identify when we are using guilt to guide our decision-making process.

If this is the case, we will often find ourselves trying to make everyone else happy, because then we won't feel guilty. In doing this, we unintentionally end up putting aside what we need and want.

If we do this too often, we will feel resentful, frustrated and in a state of blame. We'll begin to feel like we are taken for granted and unappreciated.

1. Identify Whether Guilt Is a Factor

Much of the time we are unaware that guilt is a driving force behind how we are making our decisions. To identify whether guilt is a factor in your decision-making process ask yourself these questions:

- Have I ever said yes to someone when I really wanted to say no?
- Have I ever agreed to do something because I didn't want to hurt the other person's feelings?

- Have I ever gone along with something because I didn't want to feel bad (guilty)?

Guilt can occur when we take on someone else's feelings. When we hold their disappointment, anger or frustrations for them.

Imagine that you are supposed to go to a friend's birthday party, but you're unable to attend. You let her know right away by leaving her a voice mail. Later in the day she calls and tells you how disappointed she is and how much it hurts her that you aren't coming. The phone call ends and you feel like complete crap. This is full-blown guilt.

Now you're at a fork in the road: you can either take on everything she said and how she is feeling as your own, or you can decide that her reaction is not yours to hold—it belongs to her—and you can stand in the fact that you did what was right for you.

If you are a people-pleaser who allows guilt to influence your decisions, the latter will feel extremely uncomfortable at first, especially if you are a person who leans towards doing everything you can to not feel guilty. As a recovering people-pleaser, I can attest that the uncomfortable feeling we get when we follow what we need and have to deal with other people's unmet expectations feels so much better and passes much faster than the uncomfortable feeling we get when we constantly put ourselves aside to please others. I encourage you to try it out.

Once you move through the initial discomfort of doing what you need and want, even if it leaves someone else reacting in a way that makes your stomach hurt, you will come out the other side feeling elated. You'll feel like, "Wow! I took the time to contemplate what I needed and wanted, I communicated it, and then I held my ground and didn't allow the other person's reaction to change my decision. I feel awesome."

Remember that other people will always have a reaction to your decisions, but you cannot control those reactions. They are not yours to worry about. That is on them. The only thing you can control is how you choose to handle it.

2. Identify When You Are Feeling Guilty

If you are a person who struggles with feeling guilty, it may be hard for you to decipher whether what you're feeling is guilt. Here are a few questions to ask to identify guilt when you're making a decision.

1. Are you worried about the other person's reaction (they might be hurt, mad, angry, disappointed, sad)?

2. Are you exhibiting physical signs (guilt will often manifest in our physical bodies as stomach issues)?

3. Are you ignoring what you really want because you don't want to feel bad?

4. Are you saying things like:

    - "I'll feel bad if I don't."
    - "It doesn't matter what I want."
    - "She'll be hurt if I say no."
    - "He'll be mad if I don't do it."
    - "It's not that big of a deal. I'll just suck it up."

If you find yourself saying yes to any of the above, then you may be making your decisions based on guilt. And if you find yourself feeling blame, controlled, and full of resentment, ask yourself, "Where am I making my decisions based on feeling guilty?"

3. Ditch the Guilt

Now that we've figured out whether and when we are allowing guilt to influence how we live our lives and make our decisions, it is time to change that and ditch the guilt in three steps:

1. Focus for a moment on the word "guilt" and think back to the last time you felt guilty.

2. Write about it.

- Who or what prompted you to feel guilty?
- What did it feel like?
- Where did you "hold" it or "feel" it in your body?

3. Say no.

If you realize that guilt is playing a role in your decision making, then I encourage you to begin to say no. If you're a people-pleaser, like I was, then start small and work your way up. Start where you feel like you can manage a no. Maybe this is you saying, "No, thank you" when someone offers you a glass of wine you don't like instead of politely choking it down.

When we say no, our tendency is to explain why we are saying no. This is unnecessary and is also the reason for a great deal of stress we feel when saying no. Instead of explaining, just say no. However, sometimes no can be expanded on with the following phrases:

- "I'm unable to commit to that, so it's a no."
- "No, thank you."
- "Thank you for thinking of me, but I won't be able to attend."
- "I'm flattered you thought of me. I'm unable to commit to doing that at this time."
- "I've decided not to volunteer again this year."
- "I really enjoyed the last time we got together. Unfortunately, I won't be able to make it this time."

If we are continually saying yes when we really want to say no, then we will be caught in a vicious cycle. My friend and guide Angela Clark calls this the sacrifice cycle. The way that the sacrifice cycle works is: We do something (the Sacrifice) expecting a certain outcome or reaction (the Expectation). When we don't experience the expected outcome or reaction, we become disappointed, angry, blaming, mad and sad, and we react to this emotion (Acting Out). Then we begin to feel bad for acting out (the Guilt), so we do something (the Sacrifice) to get rid of the guilty feeling, and the cycle starts all over again.

This sacrifice cycle used to be prevalent in my life. The first time I realized that I was unconsciously entering into the sacrifice cycle was on Jaye's birthday. I wanted to do something nice for him, so I made a big lasagna dinner with and a beautiful birthday cake. This was my Sacrifice. I spent all day planning the meal, getting the ingredients, preparing the dinner and decorating the cake. My Expectation was that he'd come home, eat the meal and say how grateful he was that I had made his birthday so special.

Well, my expectations weren't met. He came home from work a bit late and sat down at the table. He kissed me and the kids hello, and I dished us all up. As he began to tell us about his day, I couldn't help but notice that he wasn't touching his food. I thought to myself, *If he doesn't eat it soon, it's going to be cold.* I waited a bit longer, watching as he pushed his plate forward. I could feel my frustration creeping in. I said, "Are you not hungry?" He looked up and nonchalantly said, "I had a late lunch." At this point, I felt the disappointment that my expectations were not met. This disappointment manifested in anger and resentment, and I began to Act Out. I stood up and grabbed his plate, throwing all his food in the garbage. I then began to loudly clean up the kitchen and tell him all the thoughts that were going on in my head. This went on for some time.

Later, I began to feel bad. How was he supposed to know that I had made a big beautiful dinner for his birthday? I began to feel extremely Guilty. This put me into a state of being ready to Sacrifice again, and the cycle continued.

People-pleasing and guilt are huge factors that make the sacrifice cycle continue. We can stop the cycle at any of the stages. First, we need to identify where this cycle is occurring in our lives. Then we can work towards stopping the cycle. Can you think of examples in your life of this cycle happening?

To stop the cycle, work on doing things because you want to, not because you are trying to please someone or because you feel guilty. Ask yourself, "Am I doing this because I want to or because I am trying to make someone happy or get a certain response from them?" If the answer is the latter, ask yourself, "What would I do if I didn't feel guilty or wasn't trying to please someone?" Now, do more of that.

I am now at a point in my life where I try to live by this mantra: "If it's not a hell yes, with no hesitation, then it's a no." This is a continual work in progress, but it helps me curb my people-pleasing tendencies that are my default.

Saying no will feel very uncomfortable at first, so be prepared! Just like with any new skill, the more you do it, and the more you experience the positive effects, the easier it becomes.

My mentor Brendon Burchard always says, "Judge after behaviour change." This addresses our human tendency to immediately dismiss a new behaviour or skill by judging it before we try it. We might do this by saying, "It won't work. It will be too uncomfortable. I won't be able to do it." I've learned that trying something new, especially something that makes me feel uncomfortable, for at least two weeks allows me to experience it, and then I look back and reflect on the change I've made. At that point, you're making an informed judgment, not a knee-jerk reaction. Give it a try!

Be gentle with yourself as you learn this new skill. You've probably been putting other people's needs ahead of your own for a large portion of your life. Changing this will take time. It will not happen overnight. So if you're trying to curb your people-pleasing, but you make a decision based on guilt, smile and be proud of yourself, because you are now aware of this tendency. Celebrate your victories—you can only change what you are aware of.

STEP 3: BECOME AWARE OF YOUR SELF-TALK

Often, we are our biggest critics. When we find ourselves saying to our beloved, "You think this about me," it is often true that we actually say those things to ourselves. It can be tricky to speak kindly to ourselves because much of our self-talk is unconscious. Pay attention to your inner dialogue and become aware of your self-talk. Amazingly, when you realize that negative self-talk is occurring, you can change it, and this change will have a huge impact on your life.

ACTION STEPS: BECOME AWARE OF YOUR SELF-TALK

Words and thoughts have a great deal of power. Take control of your self-talk and channel the power of words and thoughts into the things you want to create. Every time you become aware that you have said or thought a negative thing to yourself, take these three steps:

1. Immediately stop the thought.

2. Say, "Cancel."

3. Replace the negative thought with a positive one.

For example, if you look in the mirror and catch yourself thinking, *Ugh, my hair is a disaster*, immediately stop the thought, say, "Cancel," and replace it with something positive like, *My hair is long and shiny*. Or if you catch yourself thinking, *I don't know what I'm doing*, immediately stop the thought, say, "Cancel," and replace it with *I am a problem solver and will figure this out*.

Negative self-talk inevitably spills over into our relationships. The same technique can be used. First, start to pay attention to how you think and talk about your relationship. Maybe the thoughts are: *See, we are always fighting. He doesn't care about me. We are never going to make it. We are so unhappy.* When you realize you have thought or said these things, immediately stop the thought, say, "Cancel," and insert a positive thought about something that you yearn for, such as, *We solve our conflict in an effective and loving way. He cares about me. We are on the journey of a strong, healthy, lasting relationship. We are happy in our relationship.*

STEP 4: BE EMPOWERED

To be empowered is to look within and learn about ourselves, about the stuff that lies under the surface. If our foundation of empowerment is weak and shaky, our life and the relationships we build upon it will be unstable.

If we do not understand ourselves, then it's difficult for us to be empowered in our lives because we are at the mercy of our reactions without insight into why we are reacting that way. Awareness of ourselves is absolutely key to having strong, stable and fulfilling relationships. If we want our relationships to be different, we have to start reacting to our relationships differently. We aren't in control of what happens in our lives, but we are always in control of how we choose to react to and perceive what happens.

We become empowered when we stop looking around for someone outside of ourselves to make us happy, and instead, we look in the mirror. We realize that this is *our* life. We are not passengers; we are the driver. We are not victims; we are in charge. If you are unhappy, it is up to you to make yourself happy. It's not your relationship, a change in circumstances, some unknown time in the future—it's you. If you feel out of control and overwhelmed, it is you who has control over this.

To be empowered is to embrace the belief that life is not happening *to* you. It is happening *for* you to learn and grow and evolve. One very useful way to become more empowered in your life is to look at what's happening in your life and relationship as a reflection of what is happening inside of you. Your external situations and experiences are your lessons that will lead you to greater self-discovery and empowerment. The more you learn about yourself, the more empowered you become in life and in your relationship.

Action Step: Be Empowered

The first step to becoming empowered in your life is to realize what the problems are that you feel you have in your life. To become aware of all the things you think and all the things you say that you believe if they changed you would feel better: "If only I had a different job. If only I had more connection with my spouse. If only my kids would listen. If only, if only, if only." Then take the first step:

1. Write down all of your "if onlys."
All of the things you list are the symptoms of the problem, not the root cause. To create a foundation of empowerment in our lives and relationships, we must dig into the root of what is causing the symptoms. We'll learn new skills and strategies to address those symptoms. Once we have discovered the root cause, the symptoms will begin to take care of themselves. We'll begin to dig into and uncover things about ourselves. Everything we do in the following steps will focus on the root cause. The root of all that happens in our lives and all that is created is *us*. We are the root, because the only thing that we have control over is ourselves. This is empowerment.

Step 5: Turn Inwards

The only thing that we have control over is ourselves. When we understand this, we fully realize that the pain, the resentment, the unhappiness and the frustrations arise when we try to control what we have no control over.

Instead of looking outside of ourselves towards external things and people to change so we can finally be happy, in this step we turn inwards and work on what we have control over—ourselves.

I can remember sitting in couples counselling with Jaye several years ago. We were at our lowest point in our relationship and it was a Hail Mary at this point. We were stuck in gridlock and neither of us was moving. If you had asked me then what the problem was, I would have given you a laundry list of all of the if onlys, mostly relating to what Jaye could do to make things better. Our counsellor, Trevor Warren of Corequest Counselling, let us each talk. Jaye blamed me and I blamed him, over and over again. At one point, Trevor said, "Right now it's like you're both standing there with one hand on your hip and the other hand with the finger pointed out in the direction of the other person." He suggested we each take a step back for a moment and turn the finger inwards. The intention was not to then go into how it's all your fault but rather to take the time to contemplate what your part is in the relationship that you are co-creating.

We are always co-creating our experiences in relationships. Each person has a part in every interaction. This is where, again, empowerment comes in. I had a huge aha moment as he said this. It was a pivotal point in my journey, when I became aware that I was pointing the finger outwards—in this case at my beloved—not only for the failings in our relationship but also for the failings I perceived in my own life. I then was putting the onus on "If only the relationship was better, then I would feel better." And "If only the relationship was better" really meant "If only Jaye would be more this and that, then I would feel better."

After this realization, I started to look at what was happening inside of me and to hold myself accountable for what I was bringing to my life and our relationship, for things to be going the way they were. After that, the awareness came very quickly. And everything began to change and transform.

Jaye definitely had a part in what was happening in our relationship, but the point was that it was no longer just his part but ours together. I felt empowered. Before I felt like I was spiraling out of control because I was trying to control something that wasn't mine to control: his behaviour, his actions, his emotions, his words. When I turned inwards and focused on what I could control, it was life changing. I finally felt like I was no longer just a passenger being dragged along in my life and relationship. Now I was the driver, who could direct her life and relationship how she wanted.

Action Steps: Turn Inwards

1. Identify Where You're Pointing Your Finger Outwards and Seek to Understand

At that same counselling session, each of us stated our side of the story. I had a very clear understanding of how I saw our lives, and he had a very clear understanding of how he saw our lives. We lived in the same house, we had the same family, we slept in the same bed and we had the exact same conversation or situation occur, but we each saw and experienced it very differently.

Jaye would say, "She's a lunatic, she's crazy."

I would say, "He doesn't care. He's checked out."

Trevor would say to each of us, "Well, that's how you see it."

I have come to understand that there is not one reality. There are many. Each person's perception will be shaped by their unique experiences in life. We each have a lens through which we see the world. A lens composed of all of our life experiences.

My old belief was that if four people were in the room and experienced the same situation, the situation was the situation. There was one reality. What happened happened, and that was that. But I have come to understand that this is not the case. If there are four people in the room, each person will experience the situation differently based on their past experiences, and this will dictate how they view the situation. Therefore, there will be four realities, not one. Each reality is real to each person. And each reality is as true and valid as the other.

Once you can wrap your head around this, it will make your life so much easier. Especially in your relationships. Once you can understand that each person you are interacting with sees the world in their unique way, through their unique lens, just as you do, you can then try to understand the other person's ways of looking at the situation. Instead of being stuck in your reality, instead of pointing your finger outward and saying, "You change," you form a willingness to step into each other's world.

a. Write in your journal situations where you are aware that you are pointing your finger outwards in your life and relationship. Now reflect on your part in those situations and what the other person's perspective might be.

2. Know Thyself
It's important that you find a way to reflect on yourself. You need to understand what your tendencies are and why you have those tendencies.

Begin by taking time to reflect on things. When a situation occurs in your life or relationship that triggers a reaction or emotion within you, ask yourself, "Why am I reacting this way? Why am I feeling this way? When have I felt like this before in my life?

Knowing thyself can become the most freeing experience, and when both partners learn to understand what makes themselves tick, the magic begins to occur.

The magic is taken to a whole new level when each partner in the relationship not only knows themselves inside and out but also has great understanding, compassion and acceptance of the other person's full self.

When we move into a place of understanding, acceptance and respect for each other, we will find ourselves in a place of relief. A place where we can be who we are and be fulfilled in our relationship as we are. No one is trying to change the other. We are co-creating a life based on each person's true essence.

3. Change Your Story
When turning inwards and learning to understand ourselves better, we need to take the time to get real about the stories we tell ourselves. About our fears, our thoughts and our beliefs. These stories are based on a mixture of old emotions and experiences that we have come to see as our identity.

As I discovered my story, I realized that I had a fear of "your opinion of me" (a.k.a. being judged). Without being aware of it, I had been living my life and making my decisions according to this deeply ingrained story wrapped around the fear of what people would think of me. Every decision I made in my life was unconsciously influenced and guided by this fear that resided outside of me. This fear was a part of my story.

I also had the old story of feeling like I wasn't enough. No matter what I did, it just was never enough. I wasn't smart enough, strong enough, domestic enough. That was the story that played in my head over and over again. Because I was unknowingly using this old story that I wasn't enough to guide my decisions, the outcome reflected it. I constantly felt like I wasn't measuring up in my marriage. Before I realized that I had this deep-seated belief inside me, I would blame Jaye and tell him that he didn't think I was enough. It didn't matter what I did, it was never enough for him. This was a true reality for me because it was a belief that I held very strongly. So no matter what he said or did, he could not change my mind.

Things started to transform when I identified that this was one of my core stories and then worked to change that story. I know now that for Jaye it was a losing battle that would have continued until I began to let go of the old story that I wasn't enough.

Changing our story is the epitome of cleaning up our side of the street. It is empowering and freeing for both ourselves and for those we have relationships with.

There are two steps to changing your story:

a. Identify Your Story

Changing our story requires us to identify it first. In the beginning, I had a difficult time figuring out my story. I kept thinking, *Nothing particularly dramatic has happened to me, so how can I have a story?* Then I was introduced to the "golden thread" concept. My old story was wrapped around never feeling like I was enough, always trying to please people and fearing other people's opinions of me. These were the golden threads of my story that were woven through my life and had a huge influence on how I showed up in the world and in my life.

To begin to identify your story, ask yourself this question:

What "golden threads," beliefs and fears, can I identify in my story?

These golden threads that are woven throughout our stories can hold us back and sabotage our lives. For example, my belief that I was not good enough and I needed to be more than I am sabotaged me because it made me try really hard to be perfect and led me to seek approval and validation from outside myself, which resulted in me holding back my truth. Being aware of our beliefs and fears allows us to learn to let go of old defensive ways and patterns. Awareness is the key to unlocking our ability to change our story.

Then we can begin to trust that we are the author of our story, and that it's a worthy story. Once I became aware of my belief that I am not good enough, I was able to work the muscles of self-acceptance. I realized that I had a pattern of people-pleasing and avoidance. I was able to stand in my story and fully own it by learning to make my opinion the one that counts. The stories we tell ourselves and the meaning we attach to them have great influence on what happens in our lives. It's essential to begin to trust that the fears and beliefs we've identified are a part of our old story. Then we can start to write a new story!

b. Write a New Story

Once we identify our old stories, it's time to own them and write a new one! The amazing thing about this life is that we are in the driver's seat. We are the author of our story. This means we can rewrite it anytime.

What does it mean to own our story? If we own our stories, we put a name to them. We understand them. We become the author of them. We begin to ask ourselves, "If we are not owning and authoring our story, then who is?"

The first step is to say to yourself, "If I am the author, then how do I want the story to read?"

Then start writing a new story about who you can be and who you are meant to be.

I started contemplating this question and soon began to realize that my story is one of learning to accept that I AM ENOUGH, just as I am. I wanted to feel confident. To no longer fear the judgment of others. To put my own needs, thoughts and values ahead of those of the people in my life, instead of believing that I was less than.

It doesn't matter what your old story is. You have the power to change it. I encourage you to write a new story with the following steps:

1. Journal about the things you would like to change in your old story.

2. Journal around this question: "If my life is a book and I am the author, how do I want the story to go?"
3. Brainstorm a series of short sentences that describe your story of the new life you want.

- How do you feel in this life?
- What are you doing in this life?
- What qualities in your life do you want to keep and what qualities do you wish your life had?
- Write each sentence in the present tense, as if it's already happening. For example:
    o "I am confident."
    o "I am happy."
    o "I have balance."
    o "I am healthy."
    o "I matter."
    o "I travel."
    o "I have a satisfying marriage."
    o "I am valued."
    o "I honour myself and others."
- Make all of your sentences positive statements. For example:
    o "I speak my truth," rather than "I don't silence myself."

Wow! I love this part. Getting to change your old story and write the new story that you want. How amazing is that? Finally:

4. Make a master list summarizing the new story you are creating and keep it where you will see if often. Every day, take five minutes to visualize what this life is like.

Step 6: Connect with Your Inner Wisdom & Speak Your Truth

We are made up of more than just our mind and our bodies; we also have a spirit. This step focuses on learning to reconnect, or connect deeper, with our spirit. Without this connection, we feel stuck, resentful and like a passenger in our own lives.

Several years ago I was hit smack in the side of the head with the realization that I couldn't hear myself. I didn't know what I thought, what I wanted or what I needed. I had let other people's (especially Jaye's) thoughts, opinions, desires and needs outweigh my own. It was sad but true—I had completely lost touch with and silenced my inner voice.

And this was playing out in my relationship with me feeling controlled and resentful. But what I realized once I started to reconnect with my inner voice was that Jaye wasn't controlling me; he was only fulfilling the role that I was asking him to. If we turn to our beloved and ask them what they think, what their opinion is, and then do what they say without contemplating for ourselves, we will often find ourselves blaming them for "controlling" us, which can lead to us feeling like we aren't enough. It is a vicious cycle.

In truth what is happening is we aren't taking the time to check in with ourselves and see what we think. And sometimes even when we do know what we think, we can't connect with our own opinions and thoughts because we have conditioned ourselves to value our beloved's point of view more. In my case, Jaye had only stepped up to the plate and given me his thoughts and opinions; it was me who chose to value them more than my own. Once I realized I was doing this, it became my mission to reconnect with myself, with my inner knowing so I could then begin to follow it.

At the beginning of this process I found it helpful to not ask for advice, opinions or thoughts until I had taken the time to figure out my own advice, opinions and thoughts. Then I was ready to converse about things I may not have thought of, instead of turning to others to guide me because I wasn't taking the time to guide myself.

ACTION STEPS: RECONNECT WITH YOUR INNER WISDOM & SPEAK YOUR TRUTH

It's okay to ask for advice, but make sure that you give yourself the room and the time to get clear about what you think and need first.

1. Recognize the Need for Silence & Stillness in Your Life

The answers to all of your questions lie within you. You can access these answers by getting still and quiet, and following this process:

a. Stop.
Stop whatever you're doing and find a quiet place where you can just be still. Give yourself time to quiet your mind. Get out of your head and move into your body.

b. Breathe.
Take a breath in and allow it to move through your body. As you continue to breathe, pay attention to what is going on in your body. What sensations are you having? What feelings are coming up?

c. Ask.
Once you're relaxed and your mind has slowed down, ask yourself the question that you are contemplating.

d. Listen.
Now listen for the answers. They will come.

2. Pay Attention to Your Instincts

Instincts are our inner voice speaking to us. They sound like, "Hummm." They are the hair that stands up on the back of our neck, or the gut feeling we have when we just know. They are the red flags we see but often ignore.

We don't need to intellectually understand what our instincts are telling us. We need to get out of our head, listen to our instincts and trust them. It's essential that we stop silencing them, because they are how we speak to ourselves, and often we can't explain why. But we don't need to explain why; we need to pay attention and take the time to contemplate the message.

Ask yourself:

- What is whispering to me right now?
- What am I ignoring that my inner knowing is trying to get me to pay attention to?
- What is the message I am meant to receive?

I attended Oprah's The Life You Want Weekend and loved how she described how our instincts work. She says our instincts will speak to us. First, they will start with a little whisper, like "Huh, something feels off here." If we decide to ignore this whisper, then we will get a stronger sign, like a pebble hitting us on the head. Maybe that looks like a clear incident that is harder to ignore. If still we do not get the message, then we will run into a brick wall. That brick wall will be a sign we can't ignore. Something that makes us stop and pay attention. Her point was that the messages we are meant to receive will keep being sent until we choose to listen.

Our instincts, inner knowing, inner wisdom, inner voice—however we decide to identify it—is always there, but if we ignore it and shut it down over and over again, it gets lost in the noise. The powerful thing is that it never goes away, so we can always reconnect with it and choose to listen to it. Once we do, it's like opening the floodgates. The more we stop to listen, trust and then act on our inner knowing, the more we will receive it and the stronger it will become.

3. Be Authentic & Speak Your Truth

After following the first two steps in this process, you will begin to hear your inner voice. It is now time to show up and speak your truth, even if your voice shakes while you do it. It is a lot less exhausting to do this than to silence your inner voice and pretend to be someone you aren't. Take off those masks and show up authentically as you. Let everything that you are wholeheartedly shine brightly—all of your strengths, quirks, uniqueness, beliefs and fears.

If you're used to silencing your inner voice and presenting a mask to the world, this step will push you way out of your comfort zone. Know that the more you speak your truth and the more you show up as your true self, the easier it becomes and the more amazing you'll feel.

Staying true to your inner knowing and speaking your truth—being your authentic self—leads to stronger relationships. When you follow these steps, your inner wisdom will shine through and show you exactly what you need in your life and relationships. Your job is to quiet the noise so that you can hear your inner wisdom, and then follow its guidance.

STEP 7: RECLAIM YOUR PERSONAL POWER

Our personal power is the source of influence that resides within us. If we look outside ourselves to make us feel better, we feel powerless. If we are "giving" our power away, either consciously or unconsciously, we are allowing our lives to be influenced by things that reside outside of us. This becomes an issue when we place more importance on the things that reside outside of us than that which is within us.

We give our power away without even being aware of it. Often we feel frustrated and resentful because we feel like our beloved doesn't care what we think. When we step back and take an inventory, it becomes clear that in many cases we are giving our power to them by constantly turning to them to find out what they think—searching for validation that what we think and feel is okay. They will fill the role we ask them to. When we are looking to someone for validation, for them to say, "Yeah, I think that's a good idea. Yeah, I think you should do that." Then we are giving our power to the need for validation. This puts a ton of pressure on a relationship. We will never truly feel validated until we can provide the validation to ourselves.

If we believe that what we think doesn't matter, or that we don't deserve something, we are giving our power away to that belief.

Here's the cold hard truth. No one is taking our power away from us. We are unconsciously giving it away. The great news is it is very empowering to realize that we can take our power back from wherever we have given it to.

We can give our power to, or invest it in, people, things, places, events, beliefs, fears, desired outcomes, expectations, someone else's reaction, old wounds or old stories we tell ourselves. We are usually doing this unconsciously.

WHERE WE CAN GIVE AWAY OUR POWER

People
Example: Looking to beloved to agree.

Things
Example: Buying clothes to feel better.

Places
Example: Avoiding an event because it is held in your hometown that holds many painful memories of not fitting in.

Events
Example: You hate weddings.

Beliefs
Example: I'm not good enough.

Fears
Example: What will they think?

Desired Outcomes
Example: Being praised for your contribution.

Expectations
Example: That you will receive a thank-you if you give a gift.

Someone's Reaction
Example: They'll be upset if I do that.

Old Wounds
Example: You were hurt in a relationship and now you avoid intimacy because you don't want to get hurt.

Old Stories We Tell Ourselves
Example: No matter what I do, I'm just unlucky in life.

To reclaim our personal power we must uncover who, what and where we have given away our personal power to. The thing is, we are usually unaware of where we are giving our power away. It takes some time to figure out.

ACTION STEPS: RECLAIM YOUR PERSONAL POWER

1. Identify Where You're Giving Your Power Away
An easy way to figure out if you have given your power to something or someone is to ask yourself this question:
   What variables am I using to make my decision?
   It can be tricky to pinpoint what variables we are using to make our decisions. Here are a few examples to get you started:

Decision: Do I want to meet my friend for a coffee date?
Giving Power to Variable: Friend's Reaction (If I say no, I might hurt her feelings.)

Decision: Should I dye my hair?
Giving Power to Variable: Old Story (I can't pull off a fun hair colour because I'm too conservative.)

Decision: Should I stay home full time with my kids?
Giving Power to Variable: Beliefs (My mom stayed home full time. I should too.)

Decision: Should I quit my job?
Giving Power to Variable: Need for Validation (What does my husband think?)

When I started to ask myself this question while making both small everyday decisions and major life-changing decisions, I discovered that I was basing many of my decisions on, and therefore giving my power to, the fear of what others would think of me.

This realization became very apparent to me one night a few years ago when I was at a Halloween party. We were all dressed up in our costumes and everyone was having a great time. I didn't know anyone very well, which always sends me into an introverted state, and all the ladies were having a dance party. Now, I love a good ol' dance party—but usually with my kids in our living room with no one watching! A couple of the women ran over to me and were pulling on my arms for me to join them. I instantly wanted to run and hide. This is where I asked myself that question: "What variables am I using to make this decision?" And the answers came flooding in. I was afraid of embarrassing myself. I was afraid of what they would think of me. Old wounds crept up. I flashed back to a high school dance where the guy I was dancing with looked at me, laughed and said, "Just follow her" while pointing to a girl next to me who *obviously* was a better dancer than me.

This awareness allowed me to identify where I had given my power away—the fear of what others would think and that old wound from almost twenty years ago. Once I realized this, I was able to reclaim my power. I pushed myself out of my comfort zone, got out on the dance floor and had an amazing time.

2. Analyze Your Decisions

Analyze five decisions or situations you have made or are in the process of making in your life. They can be small everyday decisions or major life-changing decisions. Follow these three steps:

1. Write down the decision/situation.
2. Brainstorm what/who is influencing your decision.
3. Use the results of your brainstorming to identify what you are giving your power to.

Here's an example:

Decision/situation: You are planning your wedding. You need to choose your bridesmaids. You have three close friends.

What/who is influencing your decision/situation: Your fiancé only has one close friend, so he wants one groomsman. If you choose only one bridesmaid, your other girlfriends will be hurt. If you have three and he has one, it will look odd.

What you are giving your power to: Your friends potential reactions (they might be hurt), people's potential judgments, your fear of being judged and standing out as different.

After you have analyzed five decisions/situations in your life, review your answers and see if patterns have emerged of where you give your power to. Once we realize where we are giving our power away, we can then begin to spot a pattern in our lives. Often, once we identify where we have given our power to in one situation, we will begin to see patterns emerge in other situations in our lives. Write them down.

3. Reclaim Your Power

After identifying and analyzing where you are typically investing your power, use the following strategies to reclaim your power.

- Close your eyes and imagine taking your power back from these beliefs, fears, people, places, situations, events, etc.
- Take a felt pen and cross off the list of beliefs, fears, people, places, situations, events that you identified you are giving your power to.
- When you become aware of basing your decisions or situations on something that resides outside of you, take time to contemplate if that fear, belief, person, need is overriding your decision and begin to question that belief or fear.
- Remember that this is a work in progress and becoming aware of where you have given your power away is the first step.
- For five minutes while looking in the mirror, say, "I take my power back from wherever I have invested it. I call my power back now."

STEP 8: PUT DOWN THE ROPE

At times in your life you will encounter power struggles. There will be situations where you find yourself in a tug-of-war with another person. Where you are on one side of the rope, pulling and saying, "No, look at it this way," and the other person is pulling and saying, "No, see it my way."

Often, in these situations you will find yourself exerting a ton of energy trying to prove that you are right. For example, that what they did to you was wrong. Or that it's time for them to admit that you are right.

My advice is to set your side of the rope down. This will immediately stop the tug-of-war. If you are no longer participating in the tug-of-war, the other person has no one to be in the struggle with.

Set your side of the rope down and remember that the only thing you have control over is how you react to a situation. Your power lies in how you decide to show up, not in trying to control what another person thinks, sees or feels.

Choose your sanity and put your side of the rope down so that you can use your precious energy for things that you can control.

* * *

Is it any surprise that the change we want to see in our relationship begins with us turning inwards and focusing on the only thing we can control—ourselves? This pillar can inspire a ton of self-awareness and can feel like we have replaced a forty-watt light bulb and with a hundred-watt light bulb. We will become aware of things we didn't see before, so as with every pillar in this book, be gentle with yourself as you see things. The point of cleaning up our side of the street is not to begin to beat ourselves up, rather it is to take care of and nourish ourselves, and to give us a deeper understanding of ourselves to empower us to create the change we want to experience in our lives.

Once we have taken the time to look inwards, we proceed to the third pillar, which turns our focus outwards to designing our ultimate relationship vision.

PILLAR 3

Design Your Ultimate Relationship Vision

"Live out your imagination, not your history."
—Stephen Covey

When we find ourselves in flux, so desperately wanting to change the trajectory of our relationship, we need to decide to do so. We need to become aware of and change old patterns. We need to try something we've never tried before because what we're used to doing just isn't working.

Turning against our beloved and telling them all the things they do that are wrong and where they are failing is only going to cause more damage. If we want change, we must consciously create the relationship we desire. Often, we are living unconsciously, just going through the motions. Our power lies in making the decision that we want something to be different. Then deciding what that looks like and taking the steps to make it happen.

First, you and your beloved must decide what your ultimate relationship vision is. What do you want your ideal relationship to look like, to feel like, to be like? This can feel daunting. To allow ourselves to dream. To imagine what our ideal relationship looks like, especially when we're in a state of gridlock and feeling hopeless.

One of the powerful discoveries Jaye and I made along this journey of designing our ultimate relationship vision was the tool of manifesting. "Manifesting" used to be a foreign term to me. I'd never really understood what it meant. Once I learned about it and wanted to begin using its powers in my life, I found manifesting to be a complete mystery and didn't know where to start.

In this pillar, I'm going to share the process that I now use to manifest my greatest desires. I use this in all areas of my life, and so can you. We'll be focusing on how to apply the process to manifesting to our ultimate relationship vision.

This process can be used daily to open you up and help you create the changes that you'd like to see in your relationship. During this process, you'll shift in awareness, gain clarity, feel energetic shifts and connect more deeply with your inner wisdom.

It's imperative to realize that this process will take time. I was inspired by the saying, "Don't expect to change something in a few days that took years to create." Hang in there. There will be days that you feel crappy. I encourage you to continue through the process to the next step, when it will all start to come together. To truly manifest change in our lives we have to move through some of the tough stuff that will come up when negative thoughts and negative energy are moving around. Keep going. The tough stuff will ebb and flow as you move towards your ultimate relationship vision.

I invite you to come along on this journey of designing your ultimate relationship vision, because if you desire change, it is up to you to make that change.

There are six steps to designing your ultimate relationship vision:

1. Do a Holistic Relationship Assessment
2. Design Your Ultimate Relationship Vision

3. Set Your Relationship Intentions
4. Identify Limiting Beliefs & Fears
5. Integrate Your Relationship Intentions
6. Trust & Ask

STEP 1: DO A HOLISTIC RELATIONSHIP ASSESSMENT

Often, when we are feeling dissatisfied in our relationship, it's hard to pinpoint why. To create a relationship where we feel fully engaged and fulfilled, it's essential to look at our relationship holistically. First, we'll do a relationship assessment to see where your relationship is at right now. That is your baseline, the place that you will move forward from as you dig into designing your ultimate relationship vision.

ACTION STEPS: DO A HOLISTIC RELATIONSHIP ASSESSMENT

Rate these areas of your relationship on a scale of 1 to 10, 1 being terrible and 10 being unbelievably amazing.

- Emotional Connection—How emotionally connected do you feel to your beloved? Quality and quantity.
- Sex Life—How satisfied are you with your sex life? Quality and quantity.
- Trust—Are you monogamous? Do you feel safe with each other, physically, emotionally and spiritually?
- Communication—Do you share important decisions? Do you communicate in a loving and effective manner?
- Forgiveness/Letting Go of the Past—Are you holding on to grudges from the past in your relationship?
- Settlement of Conflicts—Do you settle conflicts with love and respect?
- Fun—Do you take the time to go out as a couple and do things that bring you joy?

- Support—Do you honour each other for who you are, even when it's different from the other person? Do you support each other's hopes and dreams?
- Finances—Do you feel financially secure in your relationship? Is money an area of tension?
- Individuality—Do you give each other room to be who you are? Are you each satisfied as individuals? Are the following areas in each person's life being fulfilled: health, friends, family, love, finances, mission, hobby, spirituality and giving back?

When we feel unhappy, restless, frustrated in our relationship, we want an improvement in at least one of these areas. Making a change begins with assessing where you are.

Your challenge is to rate these areas of your relationship and ask yourself these questions:

- Where are we in each area?
- Is that where we want to be?
- Where do we want to be?
- What are we going to do to get to where we want to be?

I encourage you to do this assessment every week to begin to build your relationship with intention.

Step 2: Design Your Ultimate Relationship Vision

To experience a deeply satisfying love relationship, we have to first know what that looks like for each of us. We have to explore all that we desire and create the vision for what we imagine. Then we'll have to have a road map to take us to that vision. The road map is the journey. The vision is what we desire to experience along that journey.

ACTION STEPS: DESIGN YOUR ULTIMATE RELATIONSHIP VISION

1. Each partner separately lists between ten and twenty top priorities for the relationship.

2. Combine the lists so that you both add ones that your partner had that you didn't. In the end, you have all the same priorities on your lists.

3. Each partner now separately rates each priority from 1 to 5, 1 being super, can't live without, important and 5 being can live with or without it.

4. Now write all your combined priorities on one sheet of paper. On one side write your name at the top, and on the other side write you beloved's name at the top. Go down the list of priorities and mark each of your ratings under your names.

5. With the final results design your ultimate relationship vision. Put the combined top-rated priority first, and so forth down the list. You might have different rating for the priorities, so as you tally the final results, write all the priorities that were rated 1 by either of you first, all the priorities that were rated 2 by either of you second and so forth.

6. Frame your ultimate relationship vision and display it in an area where you'll both see it regularly.

Here's ours:

JAYE AND CHERYL'S RELATIONSHIP VISION

- We connect regularly.
- We have lots of great sex and intimacy.
- We settle conflicts in a loving and caring way. We talk instead of shout. We respond to each other.

- We have lots of fun. We laugh.
- We spend time as a family.
- We are monogamous.
- We trust each other.
- We are involved, loving parents.
- We treat each other with love and respect.
- We support each other's hopes and dreams.
- We love each other unconditionally.
- We are both satisfied as individuals.
- We share important decisions.
- We work well together as parents.
- We feel safe with each other.
- We live our way without worrying about other people's opinions.
- We stay active and eat healthy.
- We are financially secure.

Your relationship vision may change at times, but mostly it'll stay the same. This vision contains your greatest desires and needs to experience a thriving and fulfilling relationship. Use this relationship vision to make sure each partner is on the same page. And return to it regularly to ensure you're still on track. Turn to it in times when you're feeling disconnected and in flux to see where things have gotten off course.

Step 3: Set Your Relationship Intentions

Intentions have great power. Setting intentions is one of my favourite things to do. I do this in my life personally, as well as in my relationship. To cement our intentions, we must first contemplate what they are.

Action Steps: Set Your Relationship Intentions

1. Identify Your Top Relationship Values

a. Begin by choosing your top three values for your relationship with your beloved. You can do this separately or together. These three words will be the theme for your relationship. They will become the filter through which you put everything you do in your relationship.

Some example values are: honour, fun, trust, acceptance, growth, joy, connection, stability, acceptance, safety, freedom, caring, respect, family, monogamy, involved, satisfying, collaborative, grounded, active, healthy, secure.

b. Choose your three values and write a paragraph about why you have picked each one.

c. Create a visual representation of each value.

2. Set Your Intentions

An intention is a specific outcome you want to experience in your relationship. What would you like to manifest and bring into your relationship? Choose one intention to focus on. Be specific. We must have a clear picture of what we'd like to bring into our relationship before we begin.

a. Write down your intention for your relationship. Use the present tense.

Some sentence starters are:
- We create…
- We attract…
- We feel…
- We now…
- We have…
- We make….

For example:
- We have a loving relationship. We honour and respect each other.
- We have sex that is intimate and mind blowing.
- We make a conscious effort to be present in our relationship.
- We make date night a priority at least once a week.
- We communicate effectively and regularly.

3. Create a Visual Representation of Your Intentions

You can do this in many ways. The idea is to have a physical representation that you can look at. You can make a vision board by cutting out pictures that represent your intention from a magazine and putting them on a big poster board. Or you could make your computer screensaver a mixture of pictures that represent your intention. Or, as I've often done, you can use a chalkboard and draw/write things that represent your intention. Whatever you do, ensure that it's a visual representation of your desired reality!

4. Write a Paragraph Describing Your Why

What keeps you going on the days that you want to give up? Write a paragraph that motivates you to achieve this intention in your relationship.

Step 4: Identify Limiting Beliefs & Fears

In the previous step, we set our intentions for the new reality we'd like to create in our relationship. This is our why—what keeps us motivated when it inevitably gets hard.

This next step is all about getting clarity and reflecting more deeply. We'll do this by identifying and beginning to clear limiting beliefs and fears that are holding us back from achieving our intentions in our relationship. Identifying and clearing these blocks at a deep level allows space for our intentions to be realized.

Sometimes, we'll be able to quickly identify what limiting beliefs and fears are blocking our ability to manifest our intentions. Other times, it will be less clear. Trust yourself as you engage in this process. Be real, be honest, dig deep and know that whatever comes up is exactly what you're meant to uncover and address.

The key with clearing limiting beliefs and fears is to acknowledge the fear and then make a decision. Remember that fear and doubt don't stop the process of manifesting your ultimate relationship vision—the only thing that does is giving up! Are you going to let the fear take your energy, or are you going to allow it to flow through you so that you can make room for new positive energy, thoughts and feelings to enter your relationship? I vote let it move through you, and in the next steps I'll show you some ways to do that.

ACTION STEPS: IDENTIFY LIMITING BELIEFS & FEARS

1. Analyze

Pull out your intention that you created above and read it. Look at your visual representation you made of your intention. Now answer these questions:

a. How do I feel about this intention I have for my relationship? Thinking about your feelings will help bring limiting fears and beliefs to the surface.

b. How is not reaching this goal or realizing this intention within my relationship affecting me?

c. What is stopping me from already realizing this intention?

2. Identify

a. Write down every single "but," doubt or negative thought you have about why your intention can't or won't manifest.

b. Close your eyes and scan your body.

- Where in your body can you feel what comes up for you when answering the questions above?
- Example: your heart, head, stomach, legs, neck, throat, chest
    - What sensations can you feel in your body?
- Example: tightness, soreness, pain, numbness, emptiness, pressure, panic
    - Write your answers down.

3. Remove

Our negative emotional experiences disturb the energy meridians that run through our bodies. Tapping is a technique that helps remove our negative fears and beliefs by quickly realigning the energy meridians, allowing healing to occur.

While focusing on the negative fear or belief, tap with your fingertips on key points on your face and body (forehead, under the eyes, under the nose, chin, behind the ears, on top of the head and on the chest).

And say: "Even though I have this fear (be specific), I deeply and completely love and accept myself."

Example: Tap on your forehead with your fingertips while saying: "Even though I have this fear that we will fail, that I will get hurt again, that it will never get better, I deeply and completely love and accept myself."

Now, while tapping under your eyes say the mantra again. Then move on to tapping under your nose, and so on.

When you have completed this series you should feel the limiting fears and beliefs fading and your intention coming more into the forefront. You'll feel peace and a knowing that despite the fear of the worst thing happening, you and your beloved will be okay. This gives you the space you need to be able to invite your intention into your relationship, as you have released the negative energy of your fears and beliefs.

Step 5: Integrate Your Relationship Intentions

In the previous step, we identified and cleared limiting fears and beliefs at a deep level, allowing space for our intentions to be realized.

In this step, we'll explore the idea that to successfully manifest our intentions for our ultimate relationship vision, we need to integrate the message of our intentions for our new reality into our subconscious. We need to integrate it into the cells of our body by really feeling it in our body.

To do this we can use visualizations, feelings and words.

Action Steps: Integrate Your Relationship Intentions

The following steps are powerful strategies for integrating your intentions and bringing the feelings into the cells of your body.

1. Visualize

Visualizing helps integrate our intentions by making these feelings we want to experience real and by connecting these feelings with the reality we want to experience. When visualizing, the body can experience the visualization as if you have actually achieved your vision—this is key.

a. Re-read your answers to the questions in the previous step.

b. Now close your eyes and ask yourself:
- What do I want to feel?
- When my intention or goal is realized, what will be different in my relationship and life?

c. Visualize the following in great detail for three to four minutes:
- What's it like when all of these things are my reality?
- What am I doing? What's different?
- How am I feeling?

Really consider all of these questions in great depth in your visualization. Go deep here and really see this in your mind. Be curious and speculate.

2. Feel It

By connecting your feelings with your body, you're providing your body with the direct experience of the way it would feel when your ultimate relationship vision is realized. Our body doesn't know if it's really happening or not.

Ask yourself:

a. When I think about how my relationship and life will be different when our ultimate relationship vision is realized, where do I feel that in my body?
Example: I feel it in my stomach. I feel it in my head. I feel it in my heart.

b. What do I feel in my body?
Example: I'm sitting up straighter. My chest is open. I feel stronger through my legs. The tension in my shoulders is gone. The tightness in my chest is gone. I feel comfortable. I feel like my body is expanding. I feel like my heart if open.

3. Use Powerful Words

The previous steps were about the powerful strategies of visualizing and bringing the feelings we want to experience when our ultimate relationship vision is realized into the cells of our body, to integrate our intentions for our new reality into our subconscious.

In this action step, we'll take the integration of our intentions a bit further. Once the message is firmly implanted in our subconscious and the cells of our body, we must put ourselves on the path to accepting the new reality. In the previous action steps, we focused on aligning the energy in our body with our new desired reality. In this action step, we align the energy of our thoughts with what we say.

You can do this by creating affirmations that align with your intention. An affirmation is a statement that declares something to be true. You may not feel that it is true right now, but affirmations are all about what you want to be true. When creating an affirmation, it may feel like you're a fraud. But this is a good thing and is an indication that you have created a very strong affirmation.

For example, an intention that you want to realize in your ultimate relationship vision might be to have a connected relationship, even though right now you may feel like you and your beloved are the furthest thing from connected. Your affirmation would be: "We are emotionally and sexually connected."

How do you write an affirmation?

- Review the work you did in the previous steps throughout Pillar 3: Create Your Ultimate Relationship Vision.
- Focus on every single "but," doubt or negative thought you wrote down about why your intention can't or won't manifest (come to be realized).
- Come up with a reason why every one of these is not true. You're going to disprove them all by illuminating them with the light of the truth.
- Write five to ten affirmations around the intentions you are working on integrating.
- Write it in the present tense in a positive form, as if it has already happened.

Example: We are... We have... We create... We attract... We expand...

When you're writing your affirmations, leave room for the universe to work it's magic by not limiting the affirmations.

For example: If your intention is to have a loving and respectful relationship, a limiting affirmation would be: "We love and respect each other in our relationship in the form of giving each other the space we need to relax and be ourselves." You can see how this puts boundaries around it. To open it up and allow room for the universe to bring your desires to you in ways you haven't even thought of, add this: *"or in the form that's in the highest interest of everyone involved."*

Here are some example affirmations:
- We are connected.
- We have loving and effective communication in our relationship.
- We have fun in our relationship.
- We love and respect each other.
- Everything I do is working beautifully in our relationship.
- The universe is working to support us, it has our back, it has thousands of ways to shower us with abundance now, and we receive them with an open heart.
- We honour each other's differences.
- We have more than enough time to create the relationship we desire.

At this point in the process of integrating your intentions for your ultimate relationship vision, the energy will be flowing in full force. The fears and limiting beliefs are beginning to be released. You may be feeling amazing, or you may be feeling really uncomfortable. With change and stepping into a new reality, things (a.k.a. "stuff") are bound to come up. Believe me, I've been there. I get it. Keep moving forward and following the steps, and you'll begin to see results.

Step 6: Trust & Ask

This is the last step, where all the pieces of your ultimate relationship vision come together. Over the first part of the process we've set an intention for the new reality we'd like to see in our relationship. We've dug into the energy in our bodies and into those doubts and limiting beliefs that show up as fear. We've learned powerful ways to bring our desired reality into our subconscious. It's now time to surrender, trust and ask for guidance.

Action Steps: Trust & Ask

1. Ask for Divine Guidance & Tune In to Your Inner Wisdom
Sometimes we get stuck in our heads. We have a to-do list a mile long and we are checking items off at rapid speed. We forget that we are fully supported by something much larger than us, and we forget to tune in to our inner wisdom. This step reminds us to take the time to consciously do that.

It's simple. Get quiet, close your eyes and say: "What inspired action am I meant to take in my relationship?"

Listen for the guidance—it'll come.

Have a pen and paper ready and write down what comes to you.

2. Create Your Daily Ritual
Use what you've learned through the steps of this process and create a daily ultimate relationship vision manifesting ritual.

This is my daily ritual:
- Tap away fear and limiting beliefs.
- Say my affirmations out loud.
- Bring the feeling into the cells of my body.
- Visualize for three to four minutes in great detail what our ultimate relationship vision looks like and feels like.
- Ask for divine guidance and tune in to my inner wisdom.

* * *

Now it's time for you to take these steps and run with them to create and manifest your ultimate relationship vision. You didn't come this far to only come this far! I'm one for trying everything I've learned. Giving it my all. I don't question what works and what doesn't. I just do everything I can and the results come—they will for you too.

Keep in mind that at times you'll feel like this isn't working, but remember: roots are forming. Everything you are doing is working. Keep going. Keep believing. Keep focusing on what you want to experience more of. Take action, follow this process for Pillar 3, and the magic will appear in your relationship.

The first three pillars of making a choice, cleaning up your side of the street and creating your ultimate relationship vision have laid the base of your relationship's foundation. From this strong, consciously built base you are ready to begin to build the next pillar of communication.

PILLAR 4

Learn Loving & Effective Communication

"Anger cannot be overcome by anger. If someone is angry with you, and you show anger in return, the result is a disaster. On the other hand, if you control your anger and show its opposite—love, compassion, tolerance and patience—not only will you remain peaceful, but the other person's anger will also diminish."

—Dalai Lama

Miscommunication is rampant in relationships and causes a great deal of destruction. It's the times when we say one thing and another thing is understood, and the times when we say nothing and quiet damage occurs.

What we say and what someone hears and understands are two different things. It's often like the children's game telephone: the first person in the line whispers something, and by the time it reaches the last person, the message has become something else entirely.

Humans have many different ways to communicate, and each person has a unique way of doing this. Sometimes it can feel like we are two people speaking two different languages, yelling at each other but not understanding what the other is saying. We can get caught in the trap of believing that we are speaking perfectly clearly and that the other person can understand our way of communicating. This assumption brings us into the dangerous territory of believing that the person we're speaking to understands everything we say, just as we intended.

The reality is that, more often than not, we are saying the same thing but in different languages; therefore, we are unable to translate and understand each other.

Jaye and I had an aha moment when we tried to communicate with a third party in the room—in this case, our counsellor. This is usually a really good way to find out if you are understanding each other or if miscommunication is occurring. Because of the unique people we are, Jaye and I really do speak different languages, which led to many miscommunications. It's not that we didn't care what the other was saying; it was that we didn't understand what the other was saying.

Enter every conversation with your beloved in the frame of mind that you are speaking different languages. Do not assume that you completely understand what they are saying and do not assume that they completely understand what you are saying.

Often, when we don't know how to communicate in an effective way, our interactions become filled with reaction, blame and frustration, getting us nowhere and leaving both parties feeling like: *What just happened?!* Raise your hand if you've ever experienced this.

This was a common occurrence in our relationship. Situations would escalate quickly because my communication style was one of reaction and blame, leaving a wake of damage in our relationship. Learning to communicate in a loving and effective way has led to amazing results in all my interactions but most importantly and most noticeably in my relationship with Jaye.

A few years ago, I had this realization: It's okay to be angry, but it's never okay to be aggressive. Jaye and I were in my car having a disagreement. The topic was one that had come up over and over again in our relationship. It was about having a discussion before making arbitrary decisions. I had not addressed what was bothering me and had let my feelings pile up. That day in the car, it all came to a head as I slammed on the breaks and watched out of the corner of my eye as Jaye's Starbucks coffee flew out of his hand and hit the dash. His body jerked forward and his eyes grew wide.

I screamed at the top of my lungs, "Get out! Get out of my car now!"

He looked at me like a deer caught in the headlights, and I could see his internal struggle. He'd been taught through our counselling to "stand in the storm"—but this was a hurricane. He held steady and calmly said, "Cheryl, I'm not going to get out of the car."

I yelled again, "Get out of my car now!"

He then tried another approach: "Do you want to calm down and come pick me up later so we can finish this?"

Looking back, this was the step I needed to take, but in the heat of the moment, instead I continued to rage with no sign of relief in sight. He didn't engage. He sat and listened and somehow, through all of that, we weathered the storm. We worked to see both of our parts. Mine—allowing problems to build up and not dealing with them before the hurricane hit. His—not hearing until the hurricane hit. Mine—allowing my anger to become aggression. I was angry. So very angry. But my aggression was not okay.

I've learned that I am a person who feels fully. I feel all of my emotions deeply—the good, the bad and the ugly. I love with every ounce of my soul, I feel joy and belly laugh with all the cells of my body, and I feel anger and sadness with all aspects of my being. I'm also a person who wears my heart on my sleeve. This is a great gift and a curse at the same time. Because of this tendency I sometimes feel like I'm bat-shit crazy.

That's how I describe the incident in the car. I can feel myself being taken over by my emotions and it's like I am standing outside my body, watching myself do and say all these terrible things. Meanwhile, I'm quietly saying internally, "Cheryl, stop. Nope. Oh, crap. Stop." But I can't stop myself. In these moments when I'm angry, I can do a great deal of damage. Much like that hurricane that rips through a town and leaves a path of destruction. My words can be damaging.

My reason for sharing this story is to show how quickly communication can go sideways. We are a work in progress; we will be triggered into heightened states of emotions from time to time. The trick is to realize that this is never a good time to have a conversation. In this pillar of communication there are two important things we need to do. First, we must learn to take time away to figure out what we want, and then we need to learn how to communicate what we want in a loving and effective way.

For me, this is a daily struggle. I find myself defaulting to my people-pleasing ways without realizing it. In my life this presents like I am so easygoing. It sounds like, "I'm good. No, it's not a big deal. Sure, whatever you want." But this starts to backfire fiercely the longer I don't take the time to check in with myself.

In this pillar we are going to learn skills to prevent our emotions from hijacking us and allowing our aggression to emerge. We are not proud of ourselves in those moments when we lose our cool. The great part is that we can learn strategies to make these moments few and far between. We'll uncover techniques to avoid spewing our emotions all over our beloved. It's up to us to find a way to better handle our big emotions so that we can communicate in a loving and effective way.

There are five steps to loving and effective communication:

1. Deal with Your Heightened Emotions
2. Return or Request Discussion
3. Have the Discussion

4. Let Go & Pay Attention
5. Use a Safe Communication Container

STEP 1: DEAL WITH YOUR HEIGHTENED EMOTIONS

When we are angry or in a heightened emotional state, our physiology begins to take over. The prefrontal cortex in our brain slows down. This is the area of the brain that allows us to collaborate, make clear decisions and moderate our social behaviour. As our prefrontal cortex slows down, our brain stem activates, putting us into survival mode. We regress to a primitive state of being. This primitive part of our brain moves into the fight, flight or freeze mode. We are asking ourselves, "Am I safe?" When this system goes off but we are not in a life-threatening situation, like it was designed for, our body still reacts as though we are because it can't recognize the difference. Our advanced reasoning skills are compromised and we lose quick access to the higher thinking part of our brains. The result? When we're angry, we're stupid, and this is no time to try to effectively communicate.

In a heightened state we tend to make bad choices and decisions. Trying to resolve an issue when we are reactive is like operating with one hand tied behind our back—it's likely to do more harm than good. We can't think, our ability to process information decreases and it becomes difficult for us to pay attention to what our partner is saying. When we find ourselves in a pattern of emotional escalation, leading to back-and-forth communication based in reactivity, it often leads to one or both partners withdrawing and shutting down. This cycle will often repeat over and over again.

In our marriage, I am the escalator and Jaye is the withdrawer. The more he withdraws, the more I escalate. And the more I escalate, the more he withdraws. It's a vicious, frustrating cycle. Especially when we didn't realize what was happening.

It's important to pay attention to your "tells" that indicate you are starting to get angry and headed to the fight, flight or freeze state.

The trick is to remove yourself from the situation before then. To pull out before the point of no return. Do this as soon as you realize you are starting to go out of control.

ACTION STEPS: DEAL WITH YOUR HEIGHTENED EMOTIONS

1. Take the Time to Calm Down

When you realize you are starting to escalate or withdraw because your emotions are becoming heightened, take the time to calm down and get clear on what you are feeling. To give yourself time to feel your emotions and release them. Then to reflect on what is being triggered inside of you and what you will deal with on your own and what needs to be communicated to your beloved. Taking the time to calm down is essential, because when you try to communicate when you are upset it usually creates further damage, and a successful outcome is extremely unlikely.

2. Remove Yourself from the Situation

When you feel heightened emotions, begin by communicating your need for a break to your beloved and remove yourself from the situation. I usually don't realize I need a break until my emotions are quite escalated, so me removing myself from the situation is often very clumsy, and I stumble. Know that, like all pillars in this book, communication requires that we are gentle with ourselves. Do your best, and that will always be good enough.

In whatever way you can manage, state that you need a break. I'm usually saying this through tears. Jaye and I use a signal where the person who needs a break puts one hand on their heart and the other out like a stop sign. It is essential for both partners to always honour the signal or request for a break.

It's important that we don't leave the conversation without setting a time to return. Otherwise, our beloved is left hanging, and this is not fair. Before you remove yourself from the situation (to go to your room or for a walk, etc.), let your beloved know that you will return at a specific time. And ensure that you return at that time. If you still feel heightened, or become heightened again when you return, request more time and set another specific time to return.

Removing yourself from the situation is an extremely powerful choice to make. Even in the moments when you want to engage in a further attack, learn how to stop and remove yourself from the situation.

3. Feel & Release Heightened Emotions

Once you have removed yourself from the situation find a safe place. I often go to the bathroom, to my bedroom or outside for a breather. And take at least thirty minutes to allow yourself to feel and release your emotion and consider what your part is. This allows you to become aware of what is happening for you and why you are feeling heightened.

We will often struggle with this step of allowing ourselves to really feel our emotions. We like to skip it because we don't like to feel the hard stuff. We can become fantastic at releasing, but if we are only releasing without allowing ourselves to feel, the emotion comes back quicker and stronger next time. To move on from the emotion we must first move through it.

The purpose of the following exercises is to allow your to feel the emotion that has come up for you—mine is usually anger, so I will use the word anger throughout these steps. If anger is not the feeling you are having, replace anger with your emotion and follow the steps.

After you feel the anger you'll then process the anger and release it by allowing it to move through and out of you. By doing these activities you allow the charge of the anger to dissolve in a safe place where it will not harm anyone else with words or actions you can't take back. Take time to walk away to move through your anger in the privacy of your own space.

a. Sit Quietly with Your Anger
Allow yourself to take some time, often as little as five minutes, to sit in the anger. Cry. Scream into your pillow. Allow your body to shake if it needs to, but sit in the feeling. This is the hardest part for me, yet it's proven to be extremely beneficial.

Make sure to dig in deep. Anger is a secondary emotion, which means it masks the more vulnerable emotions that are underlying it. For example, we may feel angry because we feel humiliated or embarrassed. Instead of humiliation showing up, it's ally anger takes the stage. Anger and aggression are defence mechanisms that we use to protect ourselves from being hurt.

b. Feel the Anger
Sit and breathe and allow yourself to feel the anger. Think about why you are angry and when you have felt this feeling before. Allow that feeling to be in your body and move through your body. Then allow it to flow out of your body to be released.

c. Tune In to Your Body
When you feel the anger coming on, tune in to your body. Where is the anger in your body? Ask to release what isn't yours. Then tune in to what remains and ask for guidance.

d. Affirm
Say, "I'm in control."
Say, "I'm good."

e. Release the Anger
Choose one or more of the following anger-releasing activities:

> i. Use Your Voice
> Scream into your pillow or into the wide-open spaces of your surroundings.

ii. Do Hi-Ya!
Stand up straight and imagine you are holding an axe and chopping wood. Now physically make the motions of chopping wood while yelling, "Hi-ya!" Do this over and over again.

iii. Move Your Body
Go for a brisk walk or a full-on run.

iv. Write
Journal about your anger. Let it all out. Use a loose-leaf piece of paper so that you can write freely. Then discard it. I love to burn it to symbolize my moving through the anger. Do not re-read this writing. You are using this exercise to release the anger. If you re-read it, you bring that energy back into your body.

v. Use Your Words
Say, "I now command that all negative energy, all anger and rage, be removed from my body, mind and energy field." Breathe in and release. Do this three times.

vi. Use Your Breath
Close your eyes and pay attention to your breath. Move into your body. Breathe in, and as you breathe out, make a loud, audible sigh. Breathe in, breathe out and sigh: "AHHHHHHHH."

Connect with the anger in your body. Visualize your breath going through your body and out your feet, taking the anger with it.

vii. Write a Letter to Your Beloved
One of the techniques you can use to release the charge of your anger is to write a letter to your beloved about why you are angry. You will not give this letter to them. This is a release letter.

While writing the letter, don't censor yourself—just let it all flow out of you. The intention of this letter is to express everything you are feeling in that moment. All the anger and frustration. Once you are finished writing, the letter burn it or rip it up and dispose of it.

This process will remove the charge of the heightened emotions so that you can communicate with your beloved in a loving and effective manner when you return.

Step 2: Return or Request Discussion

Once you've taken the time to calm down, removed yourself from the situation, and felt and released your heightened emotions, you should find yourself in a state ready to return to have a discussion. This calming down time can take from thirty minutes to a few days depending on the situation. Take as much time as you need—just be sure to communicate to your beloved how long you will require and if you need to extend that time.

Action Steps: Return or Request a Discussion

1. Visualize
Before you return or request a discussion with your beloved, take some time to visualize the way you would like the conversation to occur. Focus on more than what will be said; also visualize the tone, the energy and the outcome of the conversation.

2. Request a Discussion
When you are ready to return or have a conversation with your beloved, ask them if they feel ready to begin the discussion again. This is a big one. Often, we are ready to talk, so we may walk into the room and just begin the conversation. It is essential to consider that it may not be a good time for the other person.

For example, you can ask: "Are you feeling ready to begin our conversation again?" Or if you have something to talk to your beloved about, say: "Is now a good time? There is something I would like to discuss." If the answer is yes, move on to the next step. If the answer is no, say: "Okay, when would be a better time?"

Step 3: Have the Discussion

When we enter into the conversation it's important to be aware of how we are speaking, especially if it is a difficult, charged topic. The conversation can escalate if we start to use attacking language.

Action Steps: Have the Discussion

1. Use Responsible Language
The best practice during conversations is to use responsible language by implementing these techniques to communicate effectively:

a. Use "I" statements:
"I feel _____ when you _____ because_____."
For example: "I feel disregarded when you forget to call and let me know you will be late because it seems like you don't care."

b. Imagine sending them love while you are having the conversation.

2. State What You Need
During the conversation, or really, always, don't expect your beloved to read your mind. They can't. No one can. They will fail and you will feel disappointed. If you are waiting for them to read your mind, you are playing games and giving your power away. Instead, state what you need. Be vulnerable, step out of you comfort zone and say a concrete, specific thing that you need.

For me, this often feels needy and desperate. Sometimes I will say to Jaye, "I just need you to tell me three things you appreciate about me." Or "I just need a hug."

I used to feel like, *What's wrong with him? What kind of person just sits there and watches someone cry and doesn't reach out and comfort her?* I waited and waited with great frustration, all the time thinking he knew what to do, he just wouldn't do it. It was an incredibly liberating moment when I realized he really didn't know what to do. He couldn't read my mind. And he was nothing like me, so he couldn't guess based on what he'd want because what he'd want in the same situation wasn't what I wanted. I realize now that I was making him jump through hoops, and if he didn't jump high enough or far enough, I'd berate him and tell him he wasn't trying hard enough. And the cycle would continue. The more I criticized him, the more he felt like he didn't understand me or know what I needed, so the less he tried. It's a hard lesson—the more I wanted something and the more I tried to get it from him, the less he was able to give, and vice versa.

These realizations showed me it was my responsibility to communicate what I needed, instead of waiting for him to read my mind and just get it. I know now that day would never have come. When I realized that he wasn't withholding, that in fact he just didn't know what to do, I had a choice—to look at this as a negative thing, an addition to the pile of reasons why our relationship wasn't going to work, or as the powerful fork in the road that we so desperately needed. The fork that led us to greater understanding of each other.

Step 4: Let Go & Pay Attention

This step in the pillar of communication is not about how to communicate effectively, but rather how to shift the energy and beliefs we have that are tainting our communication with our beloved.

What is our beloved doing that we are not giving them credit for? We can often slip into the dangerous zone of focusing on the areas where our beloved isn't stepping up, where they aren't doing enough, where they are falling short. Then we can find ourselves in a state of helplessness and frustration, feeling like they don't care, they aren't in this, so what am I doing here? If you find yourself saying, "My beloved doesn't care. They never put in any effort." Stop and check yourself. We need to be careful with those catch-all, overstated words like "always" and "never." This is a dangerous place to reside. It leaves us feeling powerless, just waiting for our beloved to step up. And we often have a list of things that need to be ticked off for us to acknowledge this stepping up.

When we have a predetermined list in our mind of items that must be ticked off for our beloved to get acknowledgement for their efforts, we will be disappointed without fail and we will experience the opposite of what we want. When everything our beloved does is met with criticism, their tendency is to stop trying. If they feel like what they're doing is not being noticed and they're failing anyway, why would they keep trying? We get into a push-and-pull dynamic in our relationship. One person is saying, "My partner isn't trying." Meanwhile, the other person is thinking, *Huh? What? I'm not trying? What about this, this and this?* The longer this gridlock goes on, the less likely it is that the person is going to continue to try.

What's the solution? To start to be aware of and acknowledge all the things your beloved is doing, because I can say with 99.9 percent certainty that it's extremely unlikely they are doing nothing. Begin to pay attention and search out the things that they are doing. Watch for every little thing and make a list. What we focus on expands. The more you focus on the little things they are doing, the more you'll notice the efforts they are putting in. And the more you notice, the more they will want to do. When both partners learn to let go and start paying attention to each other's efforts, each person will put in even more effort.

Action Steps: Let Go & Pay Attention

1. Identify Their Efforts

a. Keep Track of Where Your Beloved Is Trying
When you become aware of something your partner does that shows they're trying, acknowledge it within your own mind first.

b. Cement It in Your Memory
One of my favourite ways to do this is to write it down so that it's concrete and I can return to it anytime to remind myself of all the effort Jaye has been putting forth.

c. Really Take It In
Really take in your beloved's efforts. I was with a friend one day and Jaye sent me a lovely little "I'm thinking of you" text. She noticed me checking it and I told her what the text was. I could see in her face that she would have loved for her husband to send her a message like that. In that moment, I realized that I was taking that text for granted. That I wasn't really taking in the significance of that text. So I stopped and allowed myself to feel it, to acknowledge it and to really cement it into my being. Too often, we focus so much on what the other person isn't doing that we miss the things we are doing.

I remember doing a check-in appointment with our couples counsellor after an intensive three-day weekend. Our counsellor turned to me and said, "Cheryl, you look frustrated and uninterested. What's going on?"

I vented, "I don't think he's trying. I've told him what I need and he just doesn't care. It's the same old, same old."

In that moment I felt Jaye slump down beside me. His face fell and he let out a little puff of air, almost like I had just punched him in the stomach. In that moment, I realized I was focusing on all the things Jaye wasn't doing and I hadn't paid attention to all the things he was doing. When I stated that he wasn't trying and he just didn't care, he felt completely defeated.

Now he says that he felt like it didn't matter what he did; he would never figure it out, so what was the point in trying. I realized I was being too hard on him. I had set the bar way too high and I wasn't allowing room for him to try. I wanted it all, now, and he better do it now and right, or forget about it. I don't think that anyone would want to try harder under those conditions.

I also wasn't the only one who was focused on what the other person wasn't doing in the relationship. Jaye was just as quick to tell me all the things I wasn't doing and to not look at the things I was doing.

We made a pact after that session to both start paying attention and focusing on the efforts we were both putting in. Then everything started to shift.

d. Thank Each Other
Thank each other regularly, every time in fact, when you notice the other person putting in effort. To make this process even more powerful, acknowledge out loud or in writing to your partner that you noticed. It can be as simple as saying, "Thank you for that."

e. Change Your Mindset and Your Expectations
Change your mindset and your expectations around the effort the other person should put in. When we stringently hold the other person to specific expectations, they can begin to feel like they're jumping through hoops. Opening your mindset to allow your partner to put effort into the relationship in ways that you may not come up with expands your definition of effort.

2. Communicate
After you identify your partner's efforts, it then becomes imperative to communicate what you each need in specific situations, instead of waiting for the other person to figure it out.

a. Take Time Away

When you feel frustrated, resentful or angry, it's important to take some time away to reflect and discover what you need. In many cases, parenting your inner child can be helpful.

Much of what I have learned regarding parenting my inner child is from Shakti Durga's book *Empowering Relationships*. She explains that we all have basic needs that have to be met so that we can exist on Earth with some degree of skilfulness and harmony.

There are eight essential needs that make up the core of being a happy person who is able to have good interdependent relationships, as opposed to co-dependent relationships.

1. Security
2. Approval
3. Authenticity and Acceptance
4. Hope and Encouragement
5. Love
6. Attention, Stimulation and Physicality
7. Sleep and Rest
8. Fun

When these essential needs go unmet for long periods of time, the inner child will end up sabotaging us in some way to get our attention, which can often be destructive to our relationships. The good news is that we don't need to look outside of ourselves to fill these eight essential needs. We are capable of nurturing our inner child so that we can meet these needs ourselves daily.

b. Identify What You Need

The list of essential needs can help you figure out which need is not being met. I like to do this by closing my eyes and asking, "What do I need?" When my mind is quiet, I am able to hear the answer. Sometimes the answer will be, "You are tired. You need a nap." This is a simple need to fulfill. Other times, the need is more complex. Often I will hear, "You need a hug." To fulfill this need for myself, I will wrap my arms around my body and give myself a hug. I will rub my arms and soothe myself. If I hear, "You want Jaye to tell you how amazing you are and how much he appreciates you," I will tell myself these things.

We have the power to fulfill these needs for ourselves. When we meet our own needs, our outer world will begin to reflect what is happening inside of us.

c. Make Your Request

Once you've identified what you need, you are ready to request this from your partner. Communicate your need with clear, concise and specific language. General statements like, "I just need some help around here!" or "I need more connection" are too open-ended and obscure. Instead, say, "Can you please make the kids lunch?" or "I need some help preparing dinner. Can you please cut up the vegetables?" Think of something specific you and your partner can do to feel connected. Say something like, "I need you to lie with me and stroke my hair for a bit." I've discovered that when I state exactly what I need, Jaye will try his very best to do that for me. It's my job to communicate with him.

STEP 5: USE A SAFE COMMUNICATION CONTAINER

The Conscious Communication Process was taught to Jaye and me by our counsellor, Trevor Warren. Use this process when you're having trouble getting something across to your beloved. You can also use it to share information in a way that ensures there are no misunderstandings.

I love this process because it provides a sacred, safe container in which to have a discussion. This process promotes a deep level of understanding and empathy for each other's viewpoints. It's extremely powerful.

There are three steps to the Conscious Communication Process:

1. Mirroring
The mirroring step helps the listener pay full attention to what the other person is saying, instead of listening just to respond, or forming their response while appearing to listen.

The speaker will use "I" language to convey their thoughts, feelings or experiences to the listener. This may sound like, "I feel... I love... I'm sad when..." The speaker should avoid all shaming, blaming or criticizing of the listener. Once the speaker is done conveying their message, the listener responds with mirroring.

The listener will "mirror" back exactly what the speaker has said by saying something like, "Let me see if I got you. What I heard you say is (and paraphrase or give a word-for-word repetition to show the listener's understanding of what they heard). The listener shouldn't try to summarize or interpret but rather stick to reflecting back as accurately as possible. This will give the speaker confidence that they've been heard.

2. Validation
After the listener has mirrored the speaker and the speaker feels fully understood, the listener can move on to validating the speaker by saying something like, "That makes sense to me because..."

The validation step allows the listener to communicate that the information the speaker is sharing makes sense from the speaker's point of view. This step is the listener validating that they understand that the speaker's perspective is true for them.

This part of the process can be difficult if the listener has a very different perspective from the speaker. It is essential to remember that the validation step is about recognizing that what your beloved says makes sense to them. Sometimes their view might be so different from yours that you may be tempted to think that they must be wrong. In communication with your beloved, creating connection and understanding is vital. Who is right and who is wrong doesn't matter. The goal here is not to agree but rather to understand.

Once we can find a way to accept that we have different perspectives and that neither person is more right than the other, the tug-of-war of who's right and who's wrong is put aside and the power of communication to seek understanding can enter our relationship. When we reach this point of being able to see our beloved's perspective, even when it differs greatly from our own, we open the door to greater love, connection and understanding.

3. Empathy

The last step is empathy. This is where the listener takes the time to imagine what the speaker might be feeling. Are they angry, sad, lonely, afraid, happy, joyful?

To increase their understanding of the speaker, the listener can venture a few guesses by asking the speaker, "I imagine you might be feeling afraid and maybe a little sad too. Is that what you are feeling?"

* * *

After the three steps of the Conscious Communication Process are complete, it's time to switch roles and begin a new cycle. This new cycle is not in response to the previous cycle's topic. It is a whole new topic cycle. For example, if in the previous cycle your beloved brought up that it's difficult when you don't call when you're going to be late, avoid the next cycle being about them not understanding the pressure you are under at work.

Action Steps: Use a Safe Communication Container

1. Request a Conscious Communication
When one person requests a conscious communication, you then agree to engage in the following process either at that moment or at a later time. If it's a future time, make sure it's scheduled to happen in a timely manner.

When entering into a conscious communication, you and your beloved agree to sit down and follow the Conscious Communication Process for thirty to forty minutes. During this time, you each commit to listen to the other without judgment and accept each other's views as equally valid as your own.

When it's time to begin the Conscious Communication Process, follow these steps:

a. Find an environment with no interruptions or distractions.

b. Set a timer for thirty to forty minutes.

c. Sit comfortably, facing each other and making eye contact.

d. Get grounded together as a couple by breathing, and remind yourselves to be calm, with no shame, blame or criticism as you speak and no judgment as you listen.

e. When speaking don't make requests for changes in behaviour, such as, "I wish you would just... I need you to... I want you to..." Simply state what your experience is now. Say things like, "It feels like you prioritize your work over our relationship," as opposed to, "I need you to make our relationship more of a priority." Asking for a change will put the listener on the defensive.

f. Use clarifiers to gain greater understanding.

- "Repeat that" if you did not hear clearly what they said.
- "Clarify that" if you did not understand what they said.
- "Summarize that" if there was too much information.

Between cycles (switching roles), follow these steps:

a. Reset by letting go of the last cycle. Let go mentally and emotionally.

b. As the speaker, be grateful that the listener is invested in hearing and understanding you.

c. As the listener, be grateful that the speaker is willing to be vulnerable and let you into their internal world.

d. Honour each other during the process and hold space for each other's perspectives. Seek to gain a greater understanding of your beloved and to connect on a deeper level.

e. Do not discuss the topics that came up for at least twelve hours.

A Sample Conscious Communication Process
Speaker: "I would like to talk about… Is that okay?"

Listener: "Yes," or "Right now isn't a good time. Seven p.m. would be better. Does that work for you?"

Begin the Conscious Communication by saying:
Speaker: "What I want you to get is… What's bothering me is…." (Keep it super simple—one sentence.)

Listener: Step 1: Mirroring—mirror the content back as exactly as you can by saying: "So what I hear you saying is…." "Did I get you?"

Speaker: Responds with "Yes, you got me" or explains what the listener understood and what they misunderstood.

Listener: Repeats back the additional and corrected information, and then checks in again with "Did I get you?" This process repeats until the speaker feels like the listener has gotten them at least 90 percent.

Listener: Step 2: Validation—convince the speaker that you appreciate their perspective by saying:
- "That makes sense to me because…"
- "I can understand that… given that…"
- "I can see how you would see it that way because sometimes…"

Listener: Step 3: Empathy—demonstrate you can imagine how the speaker might be feeling by saying:
- "I imagine you might be feeling…"
- "I wonder if that might make you feel…"
- Check your understanding by saying, "Did I get you?"

Speaker: Responds with "Yes, you got me" or explains to the listener what they missed or misunderstood.

Listener: Repeats back the corrected information. "Did I get you?"

The Conscious Communication Process is complete once the speaker feels that the listener has fully got them and says, "Yes, you got me."

Now it is the other person's turn. They begin by saying, "Something I need you to get is…." The only thing to remember here is that their topic cannot be related to the topic that the other partner just spoke of. There is a twenty-four-hour non-referencing period. This allows for the sacred container to be maintained.

Go back and forth as many times as you are able to within the timeframe agreed to. Sometimes you'll find you move through topics quickly and gain understanding of each other easily, and other times you may find that it take you the entire thirty to forty minutes to fully understand one specific issue.

This process is powerful and can help you move through easy, breezy things as well as the big, hard issues. Remember, the point of this process is to gain understanding of each other. The goal is not to agree; it's to see the issue being addressed from your beloved's perspective.

* * *

Communication is essential in our relationships. Conflict is inevitable; it can't be avoided or controlled. What we can control is how we handle the conflict and how we communicate. If we cannot communicate lovingly and effectively with our beloved, then we will experience many misunderstandings. It will feel like we are speaking different languages, but the truth is that in a way we are. So it's important to slow down and have processes in place to ensure we fully understand what the other person is communicating.

Like all the relationship revival pillars, communication is a skill. The more you practice it and try different approaches, the better you'll become at it. Most importantly, even if you stumble, it's imperative that you keep trying to communicate in your relationship. Our beloved cannot read our mind. In the building of a strong, connected and fulfilling relationship, it is our job to communicate.

With the pillar of communication, your relationship's foundation is becoming stronger and more stable. Now it's time to build the fifth pillar, of emotional connection, to foster a fulfilling intimate relationship.

PILLAR 5

Create Your Emotional Connection

"I define connection as the energy that exists between people when they feel seen, heard, and valued; when they can give and receive without judgment; and when they derive sustenance and strength from the relationship."

—Brené Brown

At the centre of a thriving intimate relationship with our beloved is a deep sense of connection. The need to know the answer to the question "Are you there for me?" is greatly ingrained. It has been found that having a strong connection is the number one determiner of a happy and stable relationship. According to clinical psychologist Sue Johnson, the importance of connection in creating a sense of security is as important for adults as it is for children. She explains that, as adults, we are wired for connection just like we had a need for secure attachment as infants. Attachment theory explains that the need for connection is a survival response and the driving force behind bonding. It's the security a baby looks for from its parent or caregiver.

Instead of disappearing as we grow into adults, the need for secure attachment evolves into the adult need for a secure emotional bond with our intimate partner. The need to know, "Are we okay? Can I relax and know that we as a couple are okay?" If our relationship lacks connection, all attempts to improve the relationships will fail. Connection underpins of the foundation of a relationship. Connection is the key.

Connection with our beloved takes time, commitment and work and can dwindle in the blink of an eye. Like most things, continuing is easier than stopping and starting again. Connection is like a muscle; the more you work it, the stronger it becomes. The more consistent and committed we are to exercising our connection, the faster we'll see results. Just like a muscle, if we stop working it regularly and consistently it will begin to weaken. The wonderful news is that at any time we can begin working the muscle of connection again, and the muscle memory will kick in and results will appear faster.

Jaye and I have focused on connection in great depth. Our pattern is to realize we have become disconnected and reconnect. Once we start to feel connected again, this crazy phenomenon continues to happen—we stop doing what we were doing to stay connected, and within a few weeks things start to fall apart again, we feel disconnected and we sit there wondering what happened.

What happened was we stopped doing what was working because we felt good. When we feel good, it's easy to slack off and not give credit to the things that are making us feel good and connected. It's funny to me that no matter how long we've been implementing our connection tools, every time we find ourselves in that place of disconnection, it isn't automatic to just pick up and begin again. We always find ourselves saying, "Okay, we are in a state of disconnection." But having the awareness of what is happening and being able to identify why we are feeling the tension, gridlock, frustration and anger is a big step in itself. For many years we were living in gridlock and didn't have any idea what was wrong. In our minds it was each other. We were in a constant state of pointing our fingers outwards at the other person. Connection became our remedy for this gridlock.

Now, our goal is to stop stopping. It hasn't quite happened yet. But we are able to quickly identify the signs when we have stopped our connection routine. Then we are quick to start again.

Anytime, either of us can say, "I feel like we have stalled. Can we jumpstart again?" Once we begin again, the benefits come quicker and faster, as our connection muscle kicks in.

I thought that once we had succeeded at our connection model it would come back with ease, which it does once we implement it again. But remembering what to implement and what works takes us time every single time we find ourselves in disconnection. We have to go through a process to re-evaluate, re-focus and re-design our connection plan. This is because our relationship is evolving; therefore, so is what we find helps us connect.

In Pillar 5, I will guide you through the construction of your own emotional connection plan. You can tweak it and change it as you go. The important part is to begin to work the muscle of emotional connection.

There are five steps to emotional connection:

1. Be Prepared for Resistance
2. Choose One & Begin
3. Be Impeccable When You're Apart
4. Daydream
5. Create Your Emotional Connection Plan

STEP 1: BE PREPARED FOR RESISTANCE

Be prepared for the possibility that one or both of you may find connection time really uncomfortable. Jaye would be the first to tell you that connection time makes him sweat. Very regularly the response he gives when I request connection time is, "Oh, you want to talk about my feeling?" (Note the use of the singular "feeling," as though he only has one.) It's not a natural thing for him to open up the emotional, connecting side of himself. I always feel grateful that he is willing to step outside his comfort zone and do these things with me.

He often uses humour when he feels uncomfortable. I used to feel like when he made a joke, it meant that he didn't want to connect. I've since realized that he does want to experience the results of connecting, but the process is very, very uncomfortable for him. He likes to say that I'm like a PhD in connecting, communicating and emotional awareness, and he's like a toddler stumbling through it all. Connecting exercises may seem like second nature to you. You may find them incredibly fun and exciting. However, participating in them may cause your beloved to feel great anxiety and extreme discomfort. Or it may be the other way around. If one or both of you is feeling that it's not natural, it feels forced, you are stumbling, your heart is racing, you are avoiding—know that this is normal. You are not alone. Be gentle with each other and try to have compassion and understanding for what the other person might be experiencing. Don't let these uncomfortable feelings be an excuse not to begin or not to continue. Just know that if you/they can find a way to push through that uncomfortable feeling and continue with connection time, the results will be worth it—and it will get easier.

ACTION STEPS: BE PREPARED FOR RESISTANCE

Be prepared for resistance from both yourself and your partner, often at different times, in different ways, for a variety of reason. Sometimes it will be yours. Sometimes it'll be your beloved's. And other times it will be both of you at once.

Deal with resistance with two steps:

Create Your Emotional Connection

1. Identify Your Forms of Resistance

Resistance shows up in many ways. It can show up in the form of finding excuses or diminishing the exercises (e.g., "This is so stupid. I don't know why we need to close our eyes and breathe for two minutes. Let's not do that one."). It can be outright admitting that you don't want to do the connection time and refusing to participate. It can be sabotaging connection time by booking over top of it. It can be avoiding connection time by just not bringing it up. This was a big one for me. My reminder would pop up on my phone and I'd ignore it. If Jaye didn't say anything about his reminder, then we would just pretend we weren't skipping connection time. Jaye and I have made an agreement that if we notice resistance taking over for one or both of us to call each other out on it (in the nicest way possible) and to quickly get back on our horse.

When you become aware that resistance is showing up and taking over, don't beat yourself up. Instead, begin working on connecting again right away.

2. Push through the Resistance

I look at resistance as a sign that what I'm doing is working. My ego is saying, "No. No. Stay the way things are. You don't need to do that. This connection thing is a waste of time." But my spirit is saying, "Keep going. It's working. Resistance, thank you for the clear sign that we're meant to continue."

Don't let resistance win. When we become aware of our forms of resistance, it's an opportunity to push through and continue. Be prepared and push past the resistance to fight for the connection you want in your relationship.

STEP 2: CHOOSE ONE & BEGIN

This step focuses on what you can do to foster emotional connection in your relationship. I'll share the exercises and routines Jaye and I have used and still use to connect. We use these as needed and at different times. I invite you to try some of them out and see what resonates most.

Choose one and begin. Design your own connection plan for times when you find yourself in a state of disconnection. It often doesn't matter what you do; it's the time and commitment you make to spend time connecting with each other on a deep level, not just staying on the surface, that makes the difference. These are your connection nuggets of gold.

Action Steps: Choose One & Begin

Choose one of the following emotional connection activities and begin to connect with your beloved:

1. Togetherness
For three minutes, sit together with your eyes closed and breathe in and out.

2. Share
For twelve minutes (six minutes each) share about your day: one positive thing, one negative thing and one thing you're grateful for.

This is not a time for conversation. While the person sharing is speaking, the other person is listening. When the person sharing is finished, the listening person says, "Thank you for sharing your day with me." And then you reverse roles.

3. Thank Your Beloved
After you've completed your connection exercises, thank your partner. This thank-you is intended to show your gratitude and to acknowledge them for participating in the connection time, sharing and being committed to the plan you've put in place together.

Say something like: "Thank you for being here with me tonight and connecting with me. Thank you for sharing about your day."

I would often say to Jaye, "Thank you for doing these exercises of connection, even though I know they make you really uncomfortable. Thank you for your commitment and for being open to trying something that doesn't come naturally to you."

4. Dyad

Set a timer for twenty minutes and sit across from each other in a comfortable position. We are usually on the couch, lounging, facing each other. The idea is to connect emotionally. There is no physical contact. Again, like the sharing exercise, there is no back-and-forth conversation. This is a very specific dialogue.

First, pick a prompt from the list below to focus on. This prompt will be used over and over again for the whole twenty minutes.

- Tell me something you love about me.
- Tell me something you appreciate about me.
- Tell me something you admire about me.
- Tell me something you love about our relationship.
- Tell me how you want to be loved.

Begin the dyad.

Person A: "Tell me something you love about me."

Person B: Take the prompt in and sit with it for a moment.

Take time to breathe and allow the response to come to you. The power of this exercise comes when you don't think too much about it and just allow yourself to feel into the answer.

Say: "Something I love about you is…"

Person A: Take in all of what person B just shared. If you feel you understand the essence of what they have said, say: "Thank you."

There is no questioning or dialogue. Only say thank you.

If Person A does not fully understand what Person B said, they can use one of the following clarifiers:

- Repeat that—if you did not hear what your partner said.
- Clarify that, or clarify the part about—if you did not understand what your partner said. In this case, the person will try to explain what they said in another way.
- Summarize that—if there was too much information shared. In this case, the person will give the essence of what they are saying.

(Jaye uses summarize with me a lot! I have a tendency to go on and on...)

Person A and Person B now switch and repeat the steps.

Alternate until the time is up.

The next exercise is for when you're ready to deepen your emotional connection further:

1. Love You Game

Answer the following questions about each other:

1. What are your favourite characteristics of your beloved?
2. What do you see as your beloved's strengths?
3. What do you admire about your beloved?
4. What do you see as your beloved's gifts?
5. What other amazing stuff do you know about your beloved?

Step 3: Be Impeccable When You're Apart

It's important to understand the damage we may be causing in our relationship when we are not with our beloved. If we spend our time apart thinking about all the things that we wish they would do, or not do, then this is where our energy will be invested when we see them. If every time we get together with a friend we bitch and complain about every little thing that our partner does that annoys us, this is where our attention will be.

ACTION STEPS: BE IMPECCABLE WHEN YOU'RE APART

1. Pay Attention
When you're not with your beloved, begin to become aware of what you're thinking about them and how you're talking about them. This is the energy you will bring to your interactions when you see them in person.

2. Identify Patterns
Try to change how you think about and talk about your beloved when you aren't with them. To change a habit we must first become aware of our current tendencies.

Begin by taking an inventory of what you're thinking and saying about your beloved when they aren't around. I like to draw a line down the centre of a piece of paper. On one side, I write everything I thought and said that was negative, and on the other side, I write everything that I thought and said that was positive.

For example:
Inventory for October 16, 2012

Negative:
- Thought about how he always leaves his clothes lying around.
- Complained to my friend about how he always bugs me and makes me the butt of his jokes.
- Thought how cold he was this morning when I stopped by his office.
- Told my friend about how he never seems to "get" me.

- Thought about how he is so different from me.

Positive:
- Thought about how he was so sweet and started my car this morning before he left.
- Shared with my friend how Jaye is such an amazing dad

When I first started taking an inventory of what I was thinking and saying about Jaye while we were apart, I discovered that it was heavily weighted in the negative column. This was affecting our relationship in how we interacted when we were together. I was stuck in this negative energy of all that he was not, and I was bringing this to all of our encounters. It was compounded by him doing the same thing about me.

Once we become aware of our tendencies we can begin to shift them.

3. Shift Your Tendencies

After taking an inventory for a few days to clearly identify a pattern, it's time to begin to change how we think and talk about our beloved while they aren't around, thereby initiating a ripple effect to change the energy that we bring to our interactions.

Every time you become aware that you have had a negative thought about your beloved, immediately stop the thought, say, "Cancel," and replace the negative thought with a positive one. For example, if you're driving in your car and you find yourself thinking about how he's always ignoring you or how he didn't kiss you goodbye this morning before he left, immediately stop the thought, say, "Cancel," and think of something positive like, *He gave me a hug last night when he came home.*

You might find yourself saying to your friend, "I know, my partner is just like that. He's always so concerned about what other people are thinking. He doesn't know how to have a good time and laugh things off. He's always taking offence to things that I would just let roll off my back." As soon as you realize you have waded into a bashing session of your partner, stop talking, think to yourself, *Cancel*, and begin redirecting the conversation to something more positive. You can begin to shift your tendencies by flipping that particular subject by saying something like, "He's such a compassionate guy who is so emotionally intelligent. I wish I had those skills. His ability to be present without having to deflect with humour is something I try to do more." Now, when you see your beloved later, instead of being in this whirlwind energy of thinking what a stick-in-the-mud he is, no matter what you say he's going to overreact and take offence, you're now entering that encounter in the energy of your compassion and honouring his strengths. What you give out you will receive. The mission is to honour our beloved as they are.

You may stumble at first as you learn this new skill, but that's okay! Don't beat yourself up. You're changing old, deeply ingrained habits. There might be some push back, as our conversations with friends used to be filled with complaining and bashing sessions about our beloveds. It will take some time to retrain these conversations to focus more on the positives.

4. Cultivate Loving Energy

When we are apart from our beloved we have a choice about how we spend our time. One of the ways to cultivate more connection and loving energy is to spend this time doing some of the following activities:

(Note: all of the following activities can be used as conversation starters with your beloved during connection time.)

a. Journal
Pick one of the following topics and write from your heart:

- What I love about my beloved...
- Our most exciting adventures together...
- How my beloved makes me feel special...
- Why I fell in love with my beloved...
- The exciting adventures I wish we would have together...

b. Make a Love List
- Make a list about your beloved using one of the following:
- Positive attributes of my beloved...
- What I could give more of to my beloved...
- The positives of our relationship...
- What I love about my beloved...

c. Write a Love Letter

You know the saying, "Distance makes the heart grow fonder"? This action step is all about tapping into that phenomenon. Do you remember those butterflies you had in the beginning? When your beloved could do no wrong? When you were immersed in the adventure of uncovering each other and sharing yourself with each other?

Jaye and I started our relationship with a quick three-day courtship and then I was off to my hometown for a month. This left great distance between us physically, but it allowed our connection to strengthen as we spent hours and hours writing letters to each other (emails, to be exact).

I was blessed to receive an old suitcase with letters that my grandma and grandpa wrote to each other while they lived apart as he worked in another city. These letters would take weeks to reach them. They'd share their daily routines, their trials and tribulations, and their homesickness for each other. These letters show the hardship they endured being apart and how this made their love stronger.

Because of the lack of ability to communicate outside of the letter writing my grandpa would wait at the bus station every single day in the hope that would be the day that Grandma and my dad would arrive for their visit. There was no way for her to contact him in time to tell him when they'd be coming, so he waited every single day. In our modern day, this anticipation is often missing from our relationships. There is no delayed gratification to allow the build-up, the distance that makes the heart grow fonder. Distance gives space for our hearts to miss each other and to open to the things that make us each special and loveable.

Even if you aren't separated from your beloved for an extended period of time use the power of your imagination to tap into the energy of distance. Take a few minutes to close your eyes and visualize being separated from your beloved for an extended period of time. Imagine how you would feel, how missing your beloved terribly would make your heart ache. Tap into that feeling of wishing with every ounce of your being that you could just talk to them for a moment, that you could just hear their voice. In the energy of this visualization, write a love letter to your beloved.

Keeping the letter for yourself has great power in connecting and cultivating more love in your relationship, but consider giving it to your beloved as a way to let this beautiful writing infiltrate your relationship on a deeper level. This is not a necessary step, but it is a way to amplify the power of this activity.

STEP 4: DAYDREAM

If you find yourself with a little free time, lie back, tap into the love you and your beloved have for each other and daydream.

ACTION STEPS: DAYDREAM

1. Transport back in time to the days when your love was beginning. Daydream about the way you met, the feelings that occurred, the adventures you had. Think of the times that you laughed and connected. Go deep into these memories of your early love story.

Remember your first kiss, the first time your bodies touched. Remember the flutter in your tummy. Let the memories to flood in and allow yourself to feel all those amazing endorphins that are produced in the initial stages of a relationship.

2. Visit your fondest memories from the journey of your love story. Settle into your daydream by conjuring up one of your favourite memories from your love story. For me this is often the memory of the day I told Jaye we were expecting our first baby. This memory always brings a smile to my face and grounds me in that love of our shared life experiences. Go deep into the memories, remembering not only what happened but also how you felt. Keep visiting your fondest memories of your beloved and allow yourself to bask in the love and connection.

3. Integrate your present moments by daydreaming about all of the amazing moments that occur each day in your love story. Like watching a film, move through the movie of the last week and month. Allow those moments that made your heart happy to enter into your awareness. Allow yourself to relive the moments, allow yourself to feel the love, peace, joy and happiness that enter your life daily. These are all the little things—like the way he squeezed your hand when he knew the sappy TV show was getting to you—and all the big things—like the way you smiled from ear to ear with pride and admiration as he walked across the stage to receive his award of recognition in his field of study. Allow the energy of these moments to be woven into the tapestry of your love story.

4. Create your ideal future by daydreaming about your plans and hopes for what's to come in your love story. Maybe in this daydream you are jet-setting away on a romantic getaway. Your hands are linked as you walk down a sandy beach. You and your beloved are laughing and joking. Your connection is strong. You can feel it in every bone of your body. Your heart is connected to your beloved's. You are experiencing joy and excitement. You honour each other and are having so much fun together. Or maybe this future daydream is about tomorrow evening, when you will be doing your connection time, sitting together smiling at each other. When you and your beloved are moving through the awkward moments with humour and grace. When you are feeling your connection growing and for the first time in a long time you are going to bed at the same time, kissing each other goodnight and expressing your love and gratitude for one another. This future daydream is yours to make the future you desire.

STEP 5: CREATE YOUR EMOTIONAL CONNECTION PLAN

This final step in the pillar of emotional connection is to create your emotional connection plan. This plan will provide you with a road map to follow so that you can bring more of what you desire into your relationship.

ACTION STEPS: CREATE YOUR EMOTIONAL CONNECTION PLAN

1. Choose Your Activities

You can begin to create your emotional connection plan with the connection exercises from Step 2: Choose One and Begin. Pick the ones that resonate with you the most. Which ones do you wish happened regularly in your relationship?

- Togetherness
- Share
- Dyad
- Love You Game

2. Schedule It In

When you and your beloved are in a state of gridlock, of disconnection, small doses of connection on a consistent basis work really well to bring you together and deepen understanding. With your beloved, schedule in fifteen minutes of connection time for each day of the week. This should be a time when you will not be interrupted, a time when the two of you are fully available and can be present for the entire fifteen minutes. Jaye and I have always scheduled our connection time once our kids are in bed. There were times, however, when the kids weren't in bed, in which case we would tell them we were having fifteen minutes of Mommy and Daddy time and to not interrupt us unless there was an emergency. Find what works best for your schedules and the age of your kids. It could be first thing in the morning before you leave for work or during lunch hour if you're both home.

Put the agreed-upon time into your schedules, assign a reminder to pop up and commit, come hell or high water, to make connection time a top priority.

3. Schedule Each Day's Activity

Now it's time to take your favourite activities and schedule them into each daily time slot. This will set you up for success. You will never find yourself saying, "What activity do you want to do? What should we do tonight?" Instead, you will know what you are doing each night.

Here's an example of one of my and Jaye's emotional connection plans:

Day One, Day Three, Day Five, Day Seven
- Togetherness (three minutes)
- Share (twelve minutes)

Day Two, Day Four, Day Six
- Dyad (15 minutes)

Don't forget to thank your partner after you complete the connection exercises.

4. Begin

You have selected your connection exercises and scheduled in your emotional connection time. You have created your emotional connection plan. Now it's time to take that leap of faith and begin to implement the plan. As always, be gentle with yourself and your beloved as you begin using these new skills.

One extremely powerful exercise to do before implementing your emotional connection plan is to write down how you are currently feeling in your relationship. What do you rate the emotional connection in your relationship? What do you desire to feel? After a few weeks of implementing your emotional connection plan, reflect on those same questions. This allows you to really integrate the changes that are happening. Often, they are so slight that we don't notice them, until we take the time to look back and see where we were and where we are now.

* * *

Disconnection is the cause of so much of the pain we experience in our relationships. As human beings, we have an innate need to love and be loved. By working to bring emotional connection into our relationship, we set ourselves up to fulfill this need. Connection can be fostered in all the little things we do. Make it a priority and watch as your connection grows deeper and stronger.

Hand in hand with the pillar of emotional connection is the next pillar of sexual connection to create strong, connected and fulfilling relationships.

PILLAR 6

Ignite Your Sexual Connection

"Eroticism thrives in the space between the self and the other."
—Esther Perel

This has been the hardest pillar of the book for me to write by far. I have sat down to start several times and then felt completely stuck. This blockage became my challenge—as Eckhart Tolle says, "a challenge forces you to go deeper... At first you may suffer, as you suffer you're forced to transcend the suffering and go deeper. This is the opportunity and need to intensify your presence, become more conscious, alert and aware... your next level self."

I don't know how to write a book about relationships without getting into the personal, and I definitely haven't been able to figure out how to write this pillar about sex without talking about my personal experience. I have been blessed with a husband who is willing to share our journey and experiences in an authentic way in the hope that others won't feel alone. If our personal experience can help someone else move through some of their pain and suffering in their relationship, then it's worth this vulnerability. My hope is that stepping into this zone of discomfort not only helps me grow but may help others grow as well.

I won't lie to you. I mean, why would I start now? I felt embarrassed about my sex life with Jaye. It wasn't non-existent, but it definitely wasn't where I knew we both yearned for it to be. I didn't really know what was happening sexually in other people's relationships, so I often felt like we were abnormal. I felt like something must be wrong, and I hid from it. As I started to explore the topic of sexual intimacy in relationships, I soon learned that sex is one of the biggest areas where couples struggle. We weren't alone. Through this journey I've realized that I'm not the only one stumbling when I talk about sex. Many people were suffering in silence and would breathe a sigh of relief as I started a dialogue about sex and relationships. Especially as I began to share that I struggled in my relationship sexually. They cautiously nodded and said, "Me too." So I dug deeper and learned that it's hard to know what's happening sexually in relationships because people aren't talking about it.

There is a spectrum of comfort zones about sex; however, generally there is much silence and inhibition around the topic of sex in our culture. We often feel embarrassed and get offended when we talk about sex.

I understand this completely because as I sit here with my fingers on the keyboard, I am hesitant to share as deeply as I have in other pages of this book. I've realized that this is because I carry shame around sex. As I write this pillar, I am venturing way out of my comfort zone. I grew up in a family that didn't talk about sex. I was taught that sex was something you saved for marriage. That if my car was parked outside my boyfriend's house overnight when I was in my early twenties, people would talk. Sex was something that was extremely taboo. To dress provocatively, and by this I mean to show any cleavage at all, would give the wrong impression. That a nice

Catholic girl would never—fill in the blank here. It was an unspoken topic. Mine was not the only household where this happens, where the topic of sex is taboo and embarrassing.

This isn't just a Cheryl thing. Shame and sex go hand in hand in our society. And this can be one of the root causes of sex dwindling in a marriage. I have learned that best way to break free from shame is to talk about it. So here I am, working to break the shame cycle in my own life and in our culture as a whole. I have started talking about sex with my beloved, with my friends and with other people I meet. I already feel the shame fading. As I write this pillar, I feel shame rear its ugly head, and I question if this is too personal, too raw. But my guidance is clear. Talk about it, share about it, and take the power of the shame away. Break free from the shackles of this taboo, of this shame, and in the meantime, experience greater sexual liberation for myself and my marriage and create a space for others to do the same.

The root cause of the problems in our relationships is disconnection. However, what is defined as "connection" varies depending on who you're ask. A classic complaint from couples that our couples counsellor hears is the woman says, "He won't talk to me," and the man says, "She won't have sex with me." Do you see the problem? In this example, the woman defines connection as emotional and the man defines connection as sexual.

This was precisely what was happening for me and Jaye. The first thing that came into my awareness as I started digging into sex was that I had started to view sex as something that happened once we were connected—and by connected, I meant emotionally. For Jaye, however, sex is his primary language of connection.

What I discovered is that connection consists of two areas: emotional and sexual. We talked about emotional connection in Pillar 4. Sexual connection consists of being physical. Often, what is occurring in our relationships is that there has been an emphasis on emotional connection. This has put sexual connection on the back burner. The result: two frustrated intimate partners who are in gridlock, waiting for their partner to give them the connection they desire before they will give the other person the connection they desire.

If we want to build a strong, nurtured, connected relationship, we need to focus on more than one area of connection. It is essential that we simultaneously connect both emotionally and sexually. They are not separate. They go hand and hand. One does not thrive without the other.

This pillar focuses on sexual connection: our bodies coming together and communicating with physical touch. Sex is the dominant dialect of this language of touch. Sex means much more than the act of sexual intercourse. It's experiencing pleasure through physical touch. This can be accomplished in many ways. When we put too much pressure on the finish line, i.e., both partners reaching orgasm, we taint this language of physical touch with pressure and expectations.

Sex is a powerful connecting agent because when we experience physical touch, especially when we take part in sex, we release powerful bonding chemicals, such as oxytocin. These chemicals act as the agents of connection. A lack of sex leaves a couple in a depleted state of these chemical releases. Sex is a powerful bonding and connection tool that is being greatly underused in many relationships.

Sexual disconnection is rampant in intimate relationships. The reasons for this disconnection are numerous and the results are painful. To build sexual connection in our relationship we must begin with exploration to increase our awareness around what is causing the sexual disconnection. Once we have identified that we can begin to change what's not serving our sexual connection. Leading us to the important step of igniting our sexual connection and reclaiming our sexual essence. To reclaim this integral, beautiful part of who we are, we must first uncover what is blocking our sexual essence from emerging fully. The action steps in this pillar are all about becoming empowered and liberated in the sexual realm of our lives. It's important to identify what's not working in our lives and to examine what self-sabotaging behaviours we exhibit and why we are behaving the way we do. These steps will focus on giving up our victim mentality and accepting our part in the sabotage of our sex life. We'll dig into where we are giving our power away to our beloved by saying things like, "He isn't—fill in the blank here. When he does, things will change." This frame of mind leaves us disempowered because the control is in our partner's hands. He must do something for things to change.

Let's begin by flipping this dynamic on its head. As we become more self-aware, we'll release old habits, thoughts and beliefs, and this will make room for us to receive more. And let's be honest, physical touch and sex should be all about allowing ourselves to give and to receive pleasure.

How we view sex has a profound effect on our relationships. Jaye and I had come so far in our relationship, yet we were still struggling in that area. It wasn't that the sex wasn't good. It was that we weren't having enough of it. I knew this was happening, I knew it wasn't feeling good, but I didn't know how to begin to untangle the web. In this pillar, I'll share with you what helped us begin to untangle the web of destruction and ignite our sexual connection.

There are six steps to igniting a strong sexual connection:

1. Explore Your Views on Sex
2. Examine Your Story about Sex
3. Identify Your Behaviours & Excuses
4. Release, Change & Heal
5. Ignite Your Sexual Connection
6. Implement Sexual Intimacy Activities

Step 1: Explore Your Views on Sex

The first step in reestablishing our sexual connection in our relationship is to dig into what our views are about sex and what shapes these views. The views we hold will differ from the views that our beloved holds. The key here is to get to know yourself and your beloved's views. Knowledge is power, and gaining greater understanding of ourselves and our beloved will lead to building a strong foundation for sexual connection within our intimate relationship.

The first time I realized the stark difference between Jaye's family and mine when it came to our views on sex was at a dinner at his parents' house. Jaye and I hadn't been dating long, so this experience was even more shocking to me. The topic of sex came up and to my surprise everyone was laughing and talking openly about it. There was some discussion and teasing around Jaye and me being intimate. I remember thinking, *Oh my God. We don't talk about sex! And we definitely don't refer to our sexual encounters in front of our parents!*

This experience pushed me way outside of my comfort zone and made me realize I was very conservative when it came to talking about sex. Jaye's family showed me a different perspective, a different way of showing up and a different way of being. I liked it. I liked the freedom. The lack of shame and pretending. I found it fascinating and I wanted to feel more like that. I'm sure that much of what attracted me to Jaye was his freeness. He was more sexually liberated than I was, and still is. He is open and goofy. He has no shame, or less shame than I do. I wonder why. Is it because he's a guy? But no, it can't just be that, because I know many men who aren't as liberated. I think it has to do with his experiences, his conditioning and who he is, innately. He embraces his sexual essence and doesn't apologize for it or pretend it doesn't exist. I admire that. To him, a body is nothing to be ashamed of.

ACTION STEPS: EXPLORE YOUR VIEWS ON SEX

1. Dig into Your Views on Sex

To really dig into our views on sex, we will approach it by looking at the three areas that shape and influence those views: society, family of origin and ourselves.

Start by brainstorming the answers to the following questions:

a. What do you see as society's beliefs, stereotypes, attitudes, biases, fears and stigmas about sex?
For example: all women are romantics and are longing for love. Whereas all men are players and fear intimacy and commitment.

b. What are your family of origin's beliefs, stereotypes, attitudes, biases, fears and stigmas about sex?
As I shared with my personal example, all families fall on a spectrum of sexual values. Some walk around naked and speak openly about sex, whereas others never speak of sex and find the topic offensive. The way we're raised has a huge impact on how we view sex.

c. What are your own beliefs, stereotypes, attitudes, biases, fears and stigmas about sex?
All of the conditioning and experiences we have had in our lives has shaped our unique viewpoint on sex. This is where we ask ourselves what parts of our conditioning we agree with and what parts we have a different viewpoint on.

2. Identify the Common Threads

Now spend some time reviewing the answers you came up with to the questions above. Answer these questions:

- What common threads can you identify in your answers to the previous three questions?
- What do you see emerge as your top three beliefs, attitudes, biases, fears and stigmas around sex?

3. Evaluate Your Views on Sex

Write down each of these top three beliefs, stereotypes, attitudes, biases, fears and stigmas. Under each statement create your own meaning around these statements, i.e., reverse them or come up with reasons why they aren't true.

For example, if the stereotype you're working with is "Women who have sex with men they are not in a committed relationship with don't respect themselves." You would reverse this by stating something like, "Women who have sex with men they are not in a committed relationship with are sexually liberated and sexually empowered, and have deep respect for their right to choose how, with whom and when they have sex.

STEP 2: EXAMINE YOUR STORY ABOUT SEX

Once you have finished the first step, you will have some realizations about your views about sex. Now it's time to begin to understand how those views, along with your experiences, have shaped the story you have about sex.

After I went through this process, I realized I had this running commentary about sex in my head that I had picked up from my childhood and from society. It went something like this: "A nice girl would never do that. Why would he buy the cow when he can get the milk for free? Don't be a slut." By listening to this commentary, I inadvertently found myself in an intimate relationship that was lacking an adequate amount of sex. This story I had wrapped around sex was sabotaging me and therefore us. Sex became this chore, a thing that only happened if everything was absolutely perfect and every single thing on my "checklist" had been ticked off.

We will begin this step by asking ourselves the following questions. Each question will help you dig into the story you have around sex so that you can understand yourself better. Knowledge is power. The more we uncover about ourselves and the way we see the world and why, the more empowered we become.

ACTION STEPS: EXAMINE YOUR STORY ABOUT SEX

1. Uncover Your Shame
Answer the following questions:

a. When was the first time I experienced sexual shame?
Take the time to go back in your memories and recall when you have felt shame around sex. This can be described as feeling embarrassed, uncomfortable, like you had done something wrong or like you needed to hide something.

When I dug into this question, the first strong memory of shame around sex was when I was about fifteen years old. I had a boyfriend who I adored and we were exploring sexually in our relationship. We did lots of making out but had not yet moved on to intercourse. One afternoon, we were in my basement and we had been wrestling. No, not naked wrestling, just play fighting. It was fun and exciting, and we were laughing and sweating and carrying on. My mom entered the basement and right away I felt like we were caught in the act—but we weren't even doing anything. Still, I felt embarrassed and ashamed. She hugged me hello and felt my heavy breathing and sweatiness.

Fast-forward to the next day after school. She picked me up and my boyfriend was getting a ride home from us. He sat in the back seat and I was in the front. As soon as the car started moving my mom said, "So yesterday when I came into the basement I feel like I walked in on something." My immediate response was complete embarrassment and shame. We hadn't been doing anything, but if we had, why was it something that I felt so ashamed about? Like I had to hide that we might be kissing or more?

b. What experiences in my life have affected my sexuality?
Dig deep into this question and look at both the little and the big things that have affected you sexually.

As I dug into this question, I realized that some pivotal moments in my life changed my experience of sex tremendously. One of my main memories was an incident that occurred when I was in my early twenties. Even as I begin to write this recollection, I can feel the shame, guilt and embarrassment rise up inside of me. These feelings tell me that I am still healing. I am continuing to reclaim my power as I write the words and say them out loud. I believe deeply in the healing power of speaking my truth. This is the first time I've ever shared this story publicly, and only recently have I talked about it with friends and family, as I finally realized that I didn't do anything wrong. No matter how deeply ingrained this belief was.

When I was in my early twenties I was in an exclusive relationship with a guy, but we weren't extremely serious. We had sex, and it was fun and exciting and enjoyable.

Fast-forward to about six months later. We were no longer dating, as I had gone home for the summer to work and he had stayed in our university town. When I returned from the summer away, we bumped into each other at a bar. We ended up chatting and having some laughs. He invited me over to hang out later that night and I went. It was easy and fun, and I was having a great time. Until everything changed in an instant. As I sat on his bed in his apartment, he smirked at me and said, "I want to show you something." I smiled and said, "Sure." He reached for his computer and opened up a video file. On the screen I saw myself and him. I had had no idea that he had set up his webcam and taped us as we had sex. As I watched this video, which was made without my consent several months before, I felt physically ill. I felt confused and upset and completely violated.

I looked at him and said, "What the hell is wrong with you? Turn that off." The look on his face now became one of confusion. He said, "What? I thought you would like that." At this point, I could feel myself getting scared. He was obviously not the guy I thought he was. I demanded to be taken home right away. The night turned from bad to worse. He wouldn't take me home. Instead, he drove me to a secluded, wooded area and parked the car. I was scared to death. More scared than I have ever been in my life. I realized that I was in a dangerous situation. I said what I needed to say to get out of there. Finally, after my stellar performance of the "cool" girl who thought it was awesome that he had made a sex tape without her consent and used it for his own pleasure for the past six months, he drove me home.

The aftermath of this incident left me feeling like I had done something wrong. The chatter in my head said, "See, Cheryl, that's what you get for sleeping around." The shame I felt was unbearable. I had great fear of my dad finding out and what he would think of his dirty little daughter who opened her legs for a guy. I reached out for counselling support at my university and the counsellor sent me to the sexual assault centre. There they had a list of perpetrators. He was on the list several times from high school onwards. Then I was angry at myself for not knowing that he was a slime ball. And the guilt of not sharing my story so that other women would not experience the same thing or worse with him has continued to haunt me. This happened more than fifteen years ago and only recently have I fully dealt with it so that I could heal and let go.

What I realized was that this experience left me with a fear of trusting men. This experience of being violated, used and hurt is deeply ingrained in my story about sex. This experience is woven into the fabric of my sexual identity with myself and in my relationship. I have trouble letting my guard down now. I pull away to protect myself. This experience claimed much of my sexual power for far too long. I am reclaiming my power from this experience: first, by identifying that it has had such a profound impact on me, and second, by releasing those feelings of shame, guilt and anger.

2. Reframe Your Experiences

Once you take the time to examine your views and experiences that have shaped the story you have about sex, it is now time to critically analyze if these views and experiences, along with the meaning you have placed on them, are still serving you. Then this step is all about reframing the parts of your story that are no longer serving you.

a. Write about how the views and experiences you have had in your life, and the meaning you have placed on them, are affecting your sexual connection with your beloved.

b. Now write about how you can reframe and shift the meaning you have attached to these views and experiences.

I've started reframing my sexual experiences with Jaye so that they aren't filtered through the lens of what happened to me back then. Jaye is my loving husband who has never hurt me like that; he is not him. I choose to ask myself, "What is real now?" Now, I'm in a loving relationship. The lens I was seeing through prevented me from taking that into account.

* * *

Our past experiences, along with a bunch of conditioning from religion, society and family, can lead us to a place of being sexually shut down. When we learn to shed these beliefs, stereotypes, attitudes, biases, fears and stigmas, and to view sex as an intimate exchange of pleasure full of fun and excitement, we can fully embrace that we are sexual beings who have been suppressed for far too long. It's exhausting to feel like you have to be in control all the time, and it's equally draining to feel erotically impoverished. We get to choose to own our sexuality and to honour the sensual side of ourselves. Shedding these old wounds and stories allows us to become sexually empowered and to let go of the behaviours and excuses we use to avoid sexual connection in our relationship.

Step 3: Identify Your Behaviours & Excuses

When sexual connection in our relationship is not where we'd like it to be, it's important to identify which of our behaviours are contributing to the lack of sexual connection. Along with our behaviours comes the use of many excuses. In this step, we'll uncover the behaviours and excuses we are using.

Often we are not conscious of these behaviours and excuses. A few years ago, I sat across from Jaye in therapy and he said, "I feel like she uses sex as a weapon."

I felt like I had been punched in the stomach. Thoughts swirled in my head: *A weapon? What? No I don't.* This response was very much grounded in my story of all the reasons why I withheld sex. Why when he reached out for me it had gotten to a point where nine times out of ten I would turn him down. I'd always have a legitimate reason that was directly related to my checklist. This conversation was the catalyst that led me to reflect on how I was behaving and why.

I realized that I was using sex as a way to control things, and our dynamic had deteriorated to the point where we were in a habitual reaction pattern. I had closed myself off so completely, and the longer I remained closed off, the less sexual I felt. If Jaye did anything that didn't feel exactly perfect to me, I would reject him. He told me I was a jigsaw puzzle, and I had too many hoops to jump through for him. I responded defensively: "I'm not a jigsaw puzzle!" But looking back, I see that I was. So much of my stuff was bubbling over. This added to the disconnection that was happening in our relationship and left me feeling like my body and, therefore, sex were the only things I had control over. This was not easy for me to wrap my head around. Before this awareness came into my consciousness, I truly believed that if only Jaye would check off all the things on my list, and then everything else that he had no control over was also checked off, then everything would fall into place and our sex life would magically rekindle. I see now that never would have happened with me holding on so tightly to my long checklist in one hand and my finger pointing out on the other.

What was happening for us is a phenomenon that happens in many relationships. When the situations that are occurring in our relationship bring forth the painful experiences of our past, we retreat. We will unconsciously do everything we can to not feel that pain. I would go to great extremes to never feel the pain of feeling used ever again. I would have a checklist a mile long and every excuse in the book so that I did not have to be vulnerable and risk being hurt. I was not consciously doing this. But by trying to protect myself from feeling disconnected, I created the disconnection I feared.

As I was in a state of using sex, and the lack of it, as a way to protect myself, and my deeply ingrained story played in my mind, my body would respond by shutting down and in return shutting Jaye out. This realization was huge. Since I was using sex as a way to protect myself, it made sense that he would feel like I was using sex as a weapon.

So much damage is caused when we unconsciously use sex against our beloved. When we become too wrapped up in our checklists to stop and ask ourselves how our beloved might be feeling. We have a choice when we become aware of our behaviours and excuses—we can use the pain of the realization to berate ourselves for not knowing better, or we can decide to take this new information and do better from now on. As Maya Angelou said, "Do the best you can until you know better. Then when you know better. Do better."

Action Steps: Identify Your Behaviours & Excuses

If we're unaware of our behaviours and excuses, we will continue to unconsciously use them. In this step, we are going to begin to become fully aware of the behaviours and excuses we are using to avoid the vulnerability that comes with going beyond our views and past experiences to build our sexual connection with our beloved.

1. Write & Become a Detective

There are many strategies we use to avoid sex. Begin by writing down all the excuses you are aware of and use most often.

When you run out of the ones that you are aware of, begin to be a detective and pay attention to what tactics you are using to avoid sex. Write them all down so that you take the power away from them, and so that they are concrete in your mind, which allows you to change these patterns.

2. Dig into Why

Next, dig deep into why you are exhibiting each behaviour and using each excuse. What was the story you had wrapped around it? What gets triggered from your story and/or beliefs?

3. Challenge the Story You Tell Yourself

Now begin to challenge the story and ask yourself if there is another way to look at it. I often chatted with a close friend of mine who helped me see outside my deeply ingrained stories and beliefs by bringing another perspective. At the same time, these chats helped me challenge the shame I felt around sex because we were talking about it openly and honestly.

Here are a few of my top avoidance tactics that I uncovered and the stories, beliefs and alternate perspectives I came up with:

a. Giving "good" reasons for the rejection.

If Jaye wanted to have sex and approached me by saying, "I'm so stressed right now. You know what would make me feel better?" Wink, wink. I would immediately respond, either internally or outwardly, with "I'm not your stress relief. That makes me feel so used. If you want stress relief, go and take care of yourself." His comment triggered my old ingrained story about being used for sex.

My reaction immediately shut him down so that I didn't have to feel "used." What I hadn't taken into account was that Jaye uses sex as a release. I realized that my husband had come to me asking for what he needed when he felt sad or stressed, and I wouldn't let him "use" me. Instead, I attacked him and withheld connection from him because of the story I had wrapped around his approach.

When we look at this situation through the two areas of connection, I'm reminded of all the times I have come to him and have requested what I needed to relieve my stress or sadness. Because my primary way of connecting is emotional, I'd ask him to talk with me, and he would. He never said, "I'm not your stress relief. That makes me feel so used. If you want your stress relieved go and take care of yourself." Yet I did that to him, over and over again.

b. He wasn't initiating in a way that turned me on.
I was using sex to control and punish because it felt like it was an area I had control over. One of the ways that I controlled was by using the excuse that he wasn't initiating in a way that turned me on.

When Jaye initiated sex by grabbing my butt or my boob, it felt invasive, but this was his way of showing he was attracted to me. When I'd say, "Put that thing away. Ugh, you just wake up like that?" It was a major rejection and he heard it like something was wrong with him. I cringe when I imagine what my face looked like at times. What he was seeing.

The more I tried to control and rejected his attempts at initiating, the more sexually frustrated he would become, and his initiation tactics would become less refined. The longer rejection goes on the more damage it will do to both the person being rejected and to the relationship. The sad part is that it wasn't about him at all. It was my own inner stuff being projected onto him.

Today, my alternate perspective is this: I feel blessed that he is attracted to me after all of these years. That he's grabbing at me and pursuing me. I had this reality check from a friend who shared the perspective of rejoicing in this dynamic because the flip side is torture. When your husband or wife used to touch you and pursue you, cuddle you and physically connect with you, but because they've been rejected for so long, they no longer try. They have shut down and they no longer reach out. She told me the pain of that is extraordinary, and she'd go back in time if she could to stop her cycle of control earlier. To change her mindset about how she viewed those advances.

The longer this rejection and withholding goes on the more damage it does. When a major human need goes unmet, it is painful, and to stop the pain we will do many things. I could see the writing on the wall. I didn't want a sexless marriage. Or a husband who felt rejected and like he wasn't enough because I was using a human need as a weapon and as a way to control because I was afraid to be super vulnerable and if something happened, like he had an affair, I would get hurt. But by rejecting him constantly, I was creating the trajectory for my fear to come true.

4. Watch Your Sex Thoughts

What we focus on expands. If we think it, it will be proven to us. So if our beliefs, thoughts and words are along the lines of, "He's using me. All he wants is sex. I'm not sexy," then this is what we will get. Our words and thoughts are powerful. We need to be diligent in watching our sex thoughts.

When these limiting thoughts sneak in and try to sabotage you, use one of these affirmations:

- I am a sexual being.
- I love sex and get pleasure from sex.
- The more I forgive, the more sexually liberated I am because I allow myself to receive.
- I own my sexuality and I own the sensual side of myself.

When you find yourself thinking negative thoughts such as, "We have a crappy sex life. All he wants is to use me. All she ever says is no, no matter what I do," try replacing them with:

- We have an amazing sex life.
- Our sex life is full of vitality and pleasure.
- We have an exciting sex life where we both feel fully honoured and satisfied.

* * *

It can be difficult to face the behaviours and excuses we are using to avoid sex. But if we keep our heads buried in the sand, everything stays the same. With our awareness, we can create the change we desire. We must decide to be accountable and self-aware to release, heal and change the old stories and beliefs that are no longer serving us if we want to experience greater sexual connection in our relationship.

Step 4: Release, Change & Heal

In the first three steps, you have created a strong base for the pillar of sexual connection. This step will give you the tools you need to begin to release, change and heal so that there is space for you to be vulnerable in your sexual connection with your beloved.

Action Steps: Release, Change & Heal

1. Forgive
To begin to release and change the energy of old stories, it is paramount that we shift the energetic charge they hold for us.

a. Think of anyone and anything that relates to sex that still gives you an emotional charge. Make a list of all of these people and situations. You can begin the list by using what you have discovered in the previous steps. It doesn't matter how little it may seem or how big it may be, if the memory holds any sort of emotional charge, make sure to add it.

b. Feel into each item on the list one at a time. Take the time to remember the incident or person and what happened. Feel into what it meant to you. Let all the emotions that are attached to these memories come up and then say:

"I'm sorry. Please forgive me. Thank you. I love you. I set us both free."

c. Keep going over each memory you wrote down until it has no emotional charge left. This is something you will have to do over and over again. Each time you feel an emotional charge come up around a memory regarding sex, go through these steps.

2. Visualize
Take some time to sit down and visualize, in as much detail as you can, how you feel when you are sexually liberated, empowered and connected. Go deep into this visualization. Take the time to feel how you are feeling in your body. How are you acting? What are you thinking? Visualize the scene of being fully sexually connected and imagine every single detail.

3. Explore

Our beloved wants to please us sexually and will rise to the challenge, but first we must get clear about what we like, need and desire. Often, when we find ourselves feeling sexually shut down, we may have trouble at first identifying what we like. Take some time to explore your sexual wants, needs and desires. Fantasize about what you would like more of and get clear about it. Explore, alone and with your beloved, to figure this part out.

* * *

Now that you have explored your views about sex, understood and reframed your stories about sex, and begun the process of releasing, healing and changing them, you're ready to ignite the sexual connection in your relationship!

STEP 5: IGNITE YOUR SEXUAL CONNECTION

Sexual connection requires anticipation and excitement. This is why the sex is often amazing in the beginning of a relationship. The anticipation of the first kiss, next date, first time getting intimate is built into the dating process. When we are in a long-term committed relationship, this anticipation and excitement are no longer built-in features. We must learn how to generate these feelings of anticipation and excitement to ignite our sexual connection in our relationship. And we must find a way to prioritize sex. As unsexy and counterintuitive as it sounds, we must schedule it into our busy, stressful, high-pressure lives.

ACTION STEPS: IGNITE YOUR SEXUAL CONNECTION

1. Take an Inventory
Answer these questions:

- What do you describe as your stronger need? Sexual connection or Emotional connection
- What do you think your beloved would describe as their stronger need? Sexual connection or emotional connection
- What is your number one complaint regarding sex in your relationship?
- What do you think is your beloved's number one complaint regarding sex in your relationship?
- What is your number one positive regarding sex in your relationship?
- What do you think is your beloved's number one positive regarding sex in your relationship?
- On a scale of 1 to 10 how would you rate sex in your relationship? What do you want sex to be rated on this scale? What would need to happen to get to that rating?
- What are your biggest excuses and most common reasons for not having sex?
- What are the biggest reasons and excuses you hear from your beloved for not having sex?
- What are the fundamental guiding beliefs and terms around sex in your relationship? For example: Sex must be spontaneous. Both of us must have an orgasm for sex to be good.

2. Bring Back the Excitement!

Now that you have a clear understanding of the inventory of your sexual connection, this step will guide you through increasing your ratings. In this step, fantasies become reality.

a. Transform someone familiar into someone mysterious.
Go outside of your comfort zone. Go on sexual adventures with your

beloved. Do some role-playing where you bring your fantasies to life. Try new and exciting things. Maybe try a boudoir photo shoot and give the pictures with a coupon on each one to your beloved for a birthday gift. Redeem for one blow job. Redeem for a lap dance. Redeem for a quickie. Redeem for sex in a place of your choosing… the list is endless.

b. Seduce your beloved.
Many people say, "But I'm in a committed relationship. I shouldn't have to seduce my partner anymore." The power of seduction never leaves. It may be even more important to seduce your long-time committed partner later in your relationship to keep the excitement alive. Who doesn't love to be seduced?

3. Become an Explorer
Talk with your partner about what you each need, like and desire. If you require more foreplay to get your juices flowing, ask for it. If he desires you to be the initiator, he should ask for it. Explore what excites both of you and do more of that.

4. Remind Yourself of What Once Was
Reminisce about how you met and what attracted you to each other. Remember the excitement, the butterflies in your belly, the anticipation of that first kiss. Bringing these memories back into your awareness, allows the energy of this time to enter your mind and the cells of your body.

5. Schedule Sex
By scheduling sex, two things happen: You create built-in anticipation because you both know that tonight is the night! You can think about it all day. If you want to build the anticipation more, send one of your boudoir pics. Or a little text about looking forward to the

night ahead. Or more! Push yourself beyond your comfort zone and play with it. See what happens.

The second benefit of scheduling sex is that there is time blocked off for it, which makes it much more likely to happen! Treat this time like you treat emotional connection time—as sacred. No matter what is going on, you are committed to your scheduled sex time.

If you have kids, try to have your scheduled time after they've gone to bed. We do this, but sometimes we aren't so lucky. So because our kids are old enough to understand, instead we communicate with them that we are going to be in our room having Mommy and Daddy time and that they are not to interrupt unless it's an emergency. They respect this and honour our privacy and alone time.

Make a sacred space where there are no interruptions and the household knows that it is your private time.

6. Create Separation & Mystery

Unwind from each other to create some separation. Although wedding invitations often say, "Come join us as two become one," this intertwining can stop connection from happening. Connection requires another person to connect with; therefore, you must be two, not one.

Take a look at where you are fusing together. If you find yourself doing everything your beloved likes and agreeing to all their requests, ask yourself, "Where have I abandoned my individuality?" "Where can I introduce some more separation into our relationship?" "How/where can I create a space between us into which desire can flow?" This can be as simple as instead of watching the hockey game with him, going to a yoga class that you love.

Igniting your sexual connection is essential to the revival of your relationship. These sexual connection exercises in the next step will jump-start this process by pushing you past your fears into the space of embracing the unknown so that you can allow yourself to be vulnerable. Without vulnerability, we will stay in sexual disconnection.

Step 6: Implement Sexual Connection Activities

Sometimes words can get in the way of connection. The following activities will help you boost your sexual connection with direct physical experiences that are fully in the moment. Choose one and begin.

Action Steps: Implement Sexual Connection Activities

1. Holding
Lie down beside each other and hold each other in the spooning position. Do 7.5 minutes one way, and then switch places for 7.5 minutes. No talking. No Sex. No Sleeping. Just hold each other. Note: Don't do this exercise in bed at bedtime. You'll fall asleep!

2. Eye-Gazing
Sit across from each other with your knees touching and look into each other's eyes for fifteen minutes. No talking, just gazing into each other's eyes. Try to connect with the deepest part of each other.

I struggle with this activity a great deal. When we get into position and then begin to look into each other's eyes, I always begin to laugh. It's my nervous tick. It makes me uncomfortable to look deeply into Jaye's eyes and to not be able to break the gazing with words. So I laugh. It takes me a few minutes to get myself into the right space. Jaye quietly holds firm in his eye gazing until I can centre myself to be fully in the moment and gaze deeply into my beloved's eyes.

I think because I struggle so much with this exercise, I also find it incredibly powerful for our connection. One of my mantras is, "The only way that you grow is by putting yourself out there with your voice shaking, your heart pounding and your knees knocking. That's where the magic happens." I have to put myself out there and push through my nervous giggles. When I feel the resistance strongly creeping in, I ask myself: "Is the pain I am experiencing now that's caused by this disconnection more painful than the pain I will feel from doing the connection exercise I am resisting?" For me, it's always more painful to stay in disconnection, so I push through.

3. Breathing

There are two ways to do this exercise. The first is to sit in a comfortable position with your knees touching (same position as for eye gazing). The second way, which I prefer, is to have one person sitting with and the other straddling their lap.

You can close your eyes or keep them open and integrate the eye-gazing activity.

Now, partner 1 begins to breathe, and partner 2 begins to breathe in as partner 1 breathes out, and then breathes out as partner 2 breathes in. It's a circle rhythm. Do this for fifteen minutes.

One night, Jaye and I had put the kids to bed and were all settled in on the couch to do our breathing exercise. He was sitting and I was straddling him. We began the exercise and, much like with the eye-gazing activity, this one makes me giggle until I get it out of my system. So I was giggling and Jaye was breathing through my giggles. Finally, I had calmed down and was fully present in the rhythm of our breathing.

Then I heard the pitter-patter of our eight-year-old's feet. He flicked on the light so quickly we had no time to react, so we continued to breathe through the chaos. He looked over at us and said, "What are you doing?"

We said, "We're breathing together."

He laughed loudly and said, "You look ridiculous." He turned on his heel and went back to bed with his glass of water.

Jaye and I both burst out laughing hysterically. I'm sure we did look hilarious. The next day, Landon asked again what we were doing and this time we had a chance to explain that it was one of the ways Mom and Dad connect. He still found it so funny and explained it in great detail to his sister. Although this was embarrassing and felt like we had been caught in that "act," I was pleased to be role-modelling a strong, connected relationship.

4. Holding Hands

The ancient art of hand-holding is often overlooked as a powerful form of connection. Hand-holding can be done anytime. Use it while you're watching TV together. When you're walking to the grocery store or driving in the car. Use hand-holding as a way to physically and intimately connect with each other every chance you get.

5. Having Sex

The previous options are all about how to build a strong sexual connection that is rooted in physical intimacy. None of them involve the act of sex. This also builds anticipation and excitement.

But for sexual connection to be strong in our relationships, it is also essential to have regular sexual intimacy. Sexual intimacy does not necessarily mean sexual intercourse, though it can definitely be included. It means being sexually intimate with your beloved on a regular basis. Kissing, making out (like you're back in high school), foreplay, oral sex, etc. They all count. The goal here is to connect physically with your beloved in a way that provides sexual pleasure and releases those strong bonding chemicals like oxytocin.

* * *

The pillar of sexual connection is essential to reviving our intimate relationship with our beloved. If all other pillars are strong and stable, but this one still needs foundation work, the relationship will feel unstable and disconnected. To reconnect sexually with our beloved, we must first identify what unconscious beliefs we hold that were sabotaging our sexual connection. Then, we must begin to change these beliefs and introduce practical action steps to reclaim our sexual connection in our relationship. Sexual connection can be full of fun, excitement and pleasure. Reground yourself in that truth and ignite the sexual connection in your relationship.

The first six pillars are forming a strong, solid foundation for the relationship you desire. With these pillars in place, you are ready to move on to the seventh pillar and begin to let go of the past.

PILLAR 7

Let Go of the Past

"If you let go a little, you will have a little peace. If you let go a lot, you will have a lot of peace."

—AJAHN CHAH

We are often told to just get over the pain and suffering we experience in our relationships. But "getting over it and moving on" isn't something that will happen quickly or easily. Our past experiences shape who we are and the way we view the world. Each of our experiences has contributed to how we show up in our lives. The goal is not to let go, move on, and get over it. The goal is to release ourselves from the stranglehold that the past has on us.

The past is a part of us and always will be. The things that were done, were done. The things that were said, were said. That cannot be changed. But we can find ways to experience more peace in our present. The past will creep in at times; it will sideswipe us when we least expect it. The goal is to honour our past experiences, allowing ourselves to feel when they come up, but find a way to prevent the past from living in our present and controlling every minute of every day.

If we don't process the past and allow the feelings to move through and out of our bodies, these past events and the emotions they trigger will always sit right below the surface. They will continually resurface, over and over again. Letting go of the past and learning to process both the deep wounds of long ago and the argument that happened yesterday is essential to having a healthy life and relationships. This will leave us feeling empowered and free from what is holding us back.

Learning to let go of the past—in particular, all the attitudes, emotions, beliefs, fears, regrets, hurt, sadness (i.e., "baggage")—that are holding us back is often the hidden key to happiness and healing in our present life, especially in our relationships. Learning to let go of the big stuff and the little things is a must if we want to make room for more wonderful things to come into our lives. Letting go not only helps us live our best life now but also paves the way for future success. If we are haunted by our past, it will affect our present and our future.

You might be thinking, *If it were that easy I'd already be doing it!* It's true, the process of letting go can be difficult at times. It requires us to leave our comfort zone of familiar situations, habits, thought patterns, false beliefs, unhealthy relationships, regrets, fears, numbing and suppressing. We tend to shy away from doing this because it can feel stressful, and it's always going to be somewhat painful.

We unconsciously work hard to not feel those feelings that the past elicits in us. We are very skilled at numbing them out and suppressing them—until they bubble to the surface and we have no choice but to face them. Usually we face those feelings for as short a time as possible until we can push them back down and ignore them again. I know from personal experience that this technique feels like it's working, but it's only a matter of time the past sneaks up on us at every turn. We can't suppress our feelings forever. We must learn to process them to be free.

Our resistance to letting go of the past is also tied up with the myths that we believe about ourselves. A part of us, whether we know it or not, is attached to our past experiences and believes that they shape who we are. We believe that if we let go, then we will lose some essential part of our identity, personality, friendships, family or parts of ourselves that we value.

The opposite is actually true. When we let go of our past, more, not less, of our personality and gifts are able to emerge. Eckhart Tolle teaches that "we often hold on to pain far beyond its ability to serve us because it gives us a sense of identity. We replay past mistakes over and over again, allowing feelings of shame and regret to shape our actions in the present."

It takes courage and conscious action to break free from the hold that our past has on us. But it's absolutely essential if we want to create a relationship where we feel empowered, joyful and connected.

We are often told, "The past is finished. Learn from it and let it go." This is much easier said than done.

But it can be done! What follows are eight steps to help you consciously release the pain of the past and experience more peace in the present:

1. Accept
2. Feel It Fully
3. Understand
4. Become Aware
5. Release
6. Forgive
7. Believe & Surrender
8. Choose Peace Within

This process can be used to release and let go of small recent disagreements and big life-defining incidents that you've been carrying around for many years, along with all the stuff in between. The type of situation you are using the process for will dictate how much time you will need to be spend on each step. Use your judgment and work through the process step by step. If it was an argument from last night, you might be able to move through the steps and release and let go quickly and completely. If it's a big life-defining incident from years ago, you might take much longer. You might find that you need to revisit steps. You might complete the process and then have the feelings, thoughts, beliefs and pain resurface again later. If this happens, complete the process again.

Our relationships are affected by past events that happened within and outside of the confines of the relationship. This process can be used for both.

Remember, this is a process. It doesn't happen overnight. To get results, you have to do the work. The work starts with the first four steps. Often, these steps are the ones we skip or ignore. But they are the most important. They lay the foundation for the process of letting go. To release ourselves from the past, we first have to face it head on. We have to feel the emotions it brings up. We have to dig into it and really understand our perspective on it and our thoughts and beliefs about it. It's imperative that we learn to become aware when past thoughts and emotions are hijacking our present. If we try to bypass these first four steps, the rest of the process will be shaky and we will not get the final results we want.

From there, the next steps are all about letting go of the past so that it no longer haunts us. We must begin to release the feelings, beliefs and thoughts that come up for us. Then we use forgiveness of ourselves and of others to let go. And finally, we surrender the past and make the decision to choose peace within.

This process of letting go of the past is paramount for having a happy, healthy and strong relationship. If we hold on to past hurts, our relationship becomes congested with painful energy, and there is no room for new energy to come in and thrive. Give yourself this amazing gift of learning the process of letting go. Use it often to create the space to invite the type of relationships you want into your life.

Step 1: Accept

Acceptance of the past, whether it happened forty years ago in childhood or just last night at the dinner table, is the first extremely important step to letting go and setting ourselves free. The past, with all its emotions, thoughts, beliefs, judgments and expectations, lives in the cells of our bodies. That's why we don't have peace. We must accept, acknowledge and face the reality of the past first before we can begin to release it. So we start this process of acceptance in with bodies and then move on to our feelings and our perceptions. We must begin at the beginning.

In his book *You Are Here: Discovering the Magic of the Present Moment*, Thich Nhat Hahn explains that in the Buddhist tradition the path to healing is linked to recognizing the existence of suffering, embracing our suffering and understanding its nature. He says, "We must get deeply in touch with suffering to develop understanding. One day, when you are looking deeply at the nature of suffering, you will see the way that leads to transformation, to healing, and to happiness; for it is precisely through touching suffering that we discover the path to healing."

Along with accepting our circumstances, it's important to remember that our past experiences do not define us. I first uttered these words of wisdom to a dear friend at the ripe age of nineteen, and years later, she shared what a powerful change in perspective that was for her. She had made a mistake that she wished with all her heart she could take back. She was beating herself up constantly. She wondered, "What was I thinking? Why did I do that? What kind of person am I?" She said, "I'm a terrible person. I deserve to be punished and to never be forgiven." Her regret was tremendous, but her pain and suffering were amplified by this belief that what she had done then defined who she was now. In that moment, when I heard her share her regret and her new definition of herself, I turned to her and said, "Friend, this is something you did. It is not something you are." In this step of acceptance, know that the things you have done and the things that have been done to you *are not who you are*. They do not define you.

I learned this lesson when my high school boyfriend cheated on me over and over again. This situation led to me defining myself by another's actions, believing I was not enough. I know now that his cheating was about him filling something that was missing in him. It was about his own "stuff." But the effect that it had on me in my late teens and early twenties was that I couldn't understand what was wrong with *me*. I soon began to define myself as not being enough in all areas of my life. I began to believe that I didn't respect myself and that I made excuses for other people and continued to let them hurt me over and over again. This step of acceptance in the process of releasing the pain of the past allowed me to realize that his actions did not define me. My response to his actions also did not define me. This was extremely empowering. Once I realized this, I was able to release the hold this past experience had on me.

Through this step of acceptance, we must first get real about the situation that occurred. We must accept that it happened, because we can't change that. And we must also remember that it is just something that happened—it does not define who we are.

Action Step: Accept

To start this process of acceptance, answer the questions below:

- What is the reality of my past?
- What are my perceptions of the past?
- How do I feel about it?

- What is my part in it?
- What is painful about it?
- What do I regret?
- What do I wish had happened?

Go into as much depth and detail as possible. Tell the truth about your reality. Don't hold back. Remember, this is the foundation of the process of letting go of the past. Go big. Get real and face the pain and suffering that this event brings up. Allow yourself to really dig deep and get honest. Keep in mind, that facing the suffering is the path to healing.

STEP 2: FEEL IT FULLY

To let go of the pain of the past, we must first allow ourselves to feel it fully. Remember that we are usually experts at numbing and suppressing our feelings. We often try to escape the pain and suffering with TV, novels, phone calls, work, drugs, food, alcohol, etc. But when we do this, the emotions still reside in the cells of our bodies. To be able to release the pain, anger, resentment, regret, bitterness, hurt and sadness, we must first accept those feelings (step 1) and then feel them.

Just because we have pushed the suffering away doesn't mean we've gotten rid of it. Using the numbing techniques is like when we tidy up the house before we have company over by shoving everything in the back closet. It might get the mess out of sight, but it's still there, just waiting for the closet door to open. This is the same as having our suffering sitting right below the surface. It haunts us because at any time, we never know when, the closet may bust open from too much pressure from the stuff behind the door or from someone opening it.

If instead we tidied up the house by donating, recycling or throwing away all the junk we no longer needed, our closet would not be busting at the seams just waiting to open.

You have the power to clean up your closet and have a space free from all the clutter of the past, but first you must fully feel the emotions that come up—the mess you have to tidy up. Allowing yourself to feel these emotions fully makes transformation possible.

Action Steps: Feel It Fully

1. Bring the Numbed & Suppressed Emotions to the Surface

a. Write a Letter
Write a letter to the person(s) involved. This will allow you to clarify your feelings and help you accept reality as it is now.

You will not send this letter to them. Remember, this step is all about you and your inner work.

In this letter, pretend you are having one final conversation with that person. Write down everything. All the good. All the bad. Do not hold back. Get it all out. Everything you wish you had said and done, how it made you feel, what you wish you could say to them but never have.

You'll know you are uncensored when the writing becomes so messy you can barely read what you have written.

b. Write across It in Red Ink
When your letter is finished, grab a red pen and in big bold letters across it write: "Please forgive me. I forgive you. I set us both free."

c. Burn It or Rip It Up
Once you have finished the letter and written across it, it's time to dispose of it. You can burn it or rip it up and flush it.

2. Care for Your Pain & Suffering
While we're feeling it fully, it's important to take the time to soothe the suffering in us. This is where we get rid of the numbing and allow the pain to come back to us so that we can take care of it. As

the pain and suffering resurface, soothe yourself in one of the following ways:

a. Write Yourself a Letter about Being There for Yourself
For example:

Dear Cheryl,

   I am here for you. I am here to support you. I know you have grief and regret in you. I can feel there are wounds. I am sorry I abandoned you for such a long time. I am back. I am here for you.

b. Validate Yourself
Say these words to yourself:

   "I am here for you. I acknowledge you. I am here for your suffering and for your pain. Your pain, your distress, I am here. I am back and I am going to take care of you."

c. Soothe Yourself
Do for yourself what you would do for your child or best friend. Hug yourself. Rub your arms. Say, "Shhh, shhh, shhh. You're okay."

d. Visualize the Pain and Suffering as an Abandoned Baby
Your fear, your suffering, your depression, your despair is that baby in you. Say, "My dear one, I have come back. I am here for you." Imagine picking up the abandoned baby, rocking and soothing them.

* * *

We need to embrace our suffering in order to soothe it, calm it and transform it. In this step of feeling it fully care for yourself and care for your pain. Be there for yourself and support yourself through feeling the pain. You are not worrying about anyone else in this step. It is 100 percent about you.

Step 3: Understand

After we have accepted the reality of the past and fully felt the pain and suffering, it is time to begin the step of understanding. This step is about looking at many different perspectives to gain greater understanding of the past. In this step, we will look at our history as if we were a third party. The goal is to look without judgment, to simply observe.

This step of understanding continues to shift our perspective to understand that the situations, patterns and people in our lives created our experiences—they did not create us. And to begin to deal with any guilt and shame that we feel from mistakes of our past. It's important that we learn the skill of acknowledging that we did the best we could with the knowledge we had at the time. And to remember that mistakes serve to make us wiser. I've heard mistakes defined as discoveries—I like this definition. Our mistakes and experiences taught us lessons. Being human is a constant learning experience. We are students and our classrooms are our relationships and experiences. We can begin to forgive ourselves and reframe the guilt and shame by shifting our understanding of the situation. Instead of asking ourselves, "What was I thinking?" we begin to ask ourselves the more important question: "What was I learning?" We are on this earth to learn, grow and evolve. Sometimes we wish that the learning, growing and evolving were less painful, but in all situations we gain wisdom.

The understanding step is the first time in the process of letting go of the past that we begin to think of others who were involved in the situation. This step requires great compassion. This is where we will begin to put ourselves in another person's shoes, which helps us open our heart to what was happening for the other person. This is where we begin to look at the other person's humanity. Often, in situations that have caused pain and suffering, we will try to protect ourselves by defining the people involved as "other," looking at them as less than, sometimes even as monsters.

If even in times when someone has hurt us, we can find a way to understand what may have been happening for them, it can help us let go. Taking time to understand what may have been going on for others is not letting them off the hook. It's allowing ourselves to gain perspective. Especially in situations where you feel wronged by someone and feel anger and blame, this step will allow you to begin to see more than just how it affected you.

ACTION STEPS: UNDERSTAND

Understanding what the experience taught you will help you develop a sense of closure.

1. Think about and write down all of the lessons you learned from this experience.
Say, "I learn from my mistakes and become a better person."

2. Release the guilt
Say, "I leave feelings of guilt behind and move forward with the wisdom and knowledge I have gained."

3. Write about your deeper understand of what was happening for the other people involved.

STEP 4: BECOME AWARE

Becoming aware of to the thoughts and feelings the past brings up for us is the next step to letting go. In this step, we'll begin to open ourselves up to recognizing when our thinking turns to negative past events. When we find ourselves thinking of negative past events, our awareness of it will defuse the negative emotions somewhat. This will allow us to bring ourselves back to the present moment. Bringing awareness to our thoughts and feelings helps us break the cycle and let go.

With awareness also comes realizing that we have a choice of which emotions and thoughts we entertain. It takes practice, but the old thoughts and feelings will begin to lose hold over us once we become aware of them and decide to no longer entertain them. We can control our thoughts and feelings, and it's incredibly empowering once we learn to manage them.

The past is gone, but every time we give entertain thoughts or feelings about it, we bring it back into the cells of our body and into the present moment. It's time to choose to stop letting the past haunt you and hijack your present life. You have control over that. You have accepted, fully felt, and understood the feelings of the past. Now it's time to free yourself from the past by dealing with the painful thoughts and emotions. Accept, understand, feel, then deal. When thoughts of the past come up, don't deny them. Consciously decide not to allow these thoughts to make a home in your mind.

Action Step: Become Aware

1. Rubber Band Technique

How do you consciously prevent negative thoughts and feelings from taking over? Notice them and then decide to see them as a relic of a dead past. When you become aware that those old painful feelings, thoughts, beliefs and memories of the past are creeping in, use the following technique:

a. Wear a rubber band around your wrist.

b. Every time you become aware of these thoughts or feelings, snap your wrist with the rubber band.

c. Say, "Cancel."

d. Replace the negative with new positive thoughts. Try one of the following:

- "I no longer dwell on past events. I see only the love in my present."
- "I let go of the past, live in the now and let the future unfold on its own."
- "I live in the present. The past is gone and no longer plays a part in my life."
- "I let go of the past hurts and open my heart to the joy of now."
- "I release my resentment towards others and take control of my life."
- "Releasing anger from the past sets me free in the present."

STEP 5: RELEASE

Releasing is the step where we consciously and actively work to let it all go. This is a doing step, so I'm going to jump right into the action steps.

ACTION STEPS: RELEASE

1. Write

Write a final letter to the person(s) about the situation. Write about the entire situation. Include all the positives and negatives.
Note: you will not send this letter; you will burn it.

2. Visualize Change

a. Take some time to get quiet. Close your eyes and imagine going back in time to the past situation that you regret.

b. Picture the scene in as much clarity and depth as possible. Who are you with? Where are you? What are your thoughts? What do you say? What do you do? What are other people's thoughts (from your perspective)? What are other people saying? What are other people doing?

c. Imagine redoing the encounter how you wish it had gone.
Go deep with this. Picture where you wish it had taken place. What you wish you had said and done. What you wish the other person had said and done.

Follow these steps:
- If you wish you had done something differently, as you visualize the situation, apologize. Say, "I'm sorry for what I said or did."
- Visualize communicating with the other people in the past situation by calmly speaking your truth in a loving way so that they can easily understand how you feel.
- At the end of the visualization, imagine forgiving and asking for forgiveness where required.

3. Visualize the Emotions Melting Away
Imagine the anger, hurt, pain, sadness and regret melting away. Visualize the emotions moving through the cells of your body and then out of your body, leaving through your hands and feet.

4. Throw the Pain Away
Go for a jog or a walk with a backpack full of rocks. As you run/walk, toss the rocks away one by one, labelling each one a part of your anger, regret, sadness, hurt and pain.

5. Refocus
When you become aware that those old painful feelings, thoughts, beliefs and memories of the past are creeping in, use the rubber band technique from step 4 to refocus.

Remember, the goal is not to deny these thoughts, feelings and memories but to rather process them. First, accept and acknowledge them—"Hi there. I see you." Then allow yourself to feel the emotions fully and completely. Now decide not to let them make a home in your mind and present moment. Instead, in this step, release them with one of the previous techniques in this step.

6. Talk to a Trusted Friend or Professional

Sometimes when we are trying to release painful emotions we will turn to a friend, counsellor, mentor or other trusted person. There is a time and a place where this can be useful. Stay aware, however, that this may be a way to avoid feeling and instead pass the hot potato to someone else. Ask yourself, "Did I feel that or was that a way to stop myself from feeling it?

7. Communicate with the Person(s) Involved

Communicating how you feel out loud or in writing can help you let go and release. Remember that you can only control how you show up. How the other person responds is out of your control. Speak your truth in a clear and kind manner and communicate what you need to say.

STEP 6: FORGIVE

Many of us have heard the expression, "Holding on to anger is like drinking poison and expecting the other person to die." It's essential that we realize that carrying bitterness, resentment and anger only burdens us. Forgiveness is the step through which we release the past and reclaim our present. When we are unforgiving, we feel stuck, weak, angry and resentful, and these low vibrational feelings block our capacity to grow, heal, move on, let go and live life to the fullest.

It's important to remember that this is not about letting the other person off the hook or condoning their actions. It is about releasing ourselves from pain. It's like being in a tug-of-war. You are holding on to one side of the rope, pulling and pulling. The other person is holding on to the rope (often knowing it), pulling and pulling.

Forgiveness can be viewed as setting down your side of the rope (like in Pillar 2). This releases you from the tug-of-war. You're saying, "I am setting myself free from this."

This step of forgiveness is about not only forgiving others for the pain and hurt they have caused us but also forgiving ourselves. We are always hardest on ourselves.

The process of forgiving is integral to releasing ourselves from the hold of the past and experiencing peace in the present.

Action Steps: Forgive

1. Release Expectations
To begin the process of forgiving, we must first release our expectations of the shoulda, woulda, couldas and if onlys that we're hanging on to.

Visualize a box in your head labelled "Expectations." Whenever you realize you are dwelling on how things should have been, mentally shelve these thoughts in the "Expectations" box. You can make this a beautiful box with a big red bow if you like.

2. Set the Intention
Set the intention to forgive others and yourself, and to ask for forgiveness for all the hurt, regret and pain.

3. Ask for Forgiveness
a. "I'm sorry, please forgive me and thank you. I love you."
Bring the person into your mind. You can sing or say this to them and/or imagine them saying or singing it to you. Also say or sing it to yourself.

b. "I forgive you, please forgive me. I forgive myself.
Visualize the person and the situation and imagine saying this.

c. Write a letter to the person(s) about everything you forgive them for and what you ask forgiveness for. Write across it when you're finished: I FORGIVE YOU. PLEASE FORGIVE ME. I FORGIVE MYSELF. I SET US BOTH FREE. Now burn it or dispose of it.

d. You can take the forgiveness step further if you desire, though it is not necessary, by having a conversation with or writing a letter to the person(s) involved and asking for forgiveness. You can also request forgiveness. Use your skills of being empowered in this step by remembering that you can only control yourself. If you choose to take this step and communicate, know that how they choose to respond is not your responsibility.

STEP 7: BELIEVE & SURRENDER

At this point in the process, you have done much of what you can to let go of the pain and suffering you feel from the past. This step comes down to believing that the universe is unfolding as it should. Things happen for a reason, and sometimes the reasons for a particular experience or decision may not be clear to us in the moment, or even years later. Now is the time to believe, to have faith and to turn your pain and suffering over to a higher power (whatever that is to you) and ask it to help you and show you the way. I love how Gabby Bernstein explains it in her book Miracles Now: "Through prayer we ask an invisible teacher to help us. Call it the Holy Spirit, God, Buddha, The Universe, A Higher Power, The Creator, Call it Love. The name doesn't matter. What matters is you choose to call on it."

No matter what your religious or spiritual beliefs are, having faith in something other than yourself can really serve you. Knowing that there is a greater purpose and perhaps meaning that you may not understand now has substantial power. You are not alone. You are fully supported. This is the time to lean on that higher support.

This step is where you surrender the pain of the past. Once you've done all you can do by accepting it, feeling it, understanding it, being aware of it and releasing it, you can turn to that unconditional support and say, "I surrender this now. Show me the way."

Action Step: Believe & Surrender

We've all heard the saying, "Ask and you shall receive." This is the premise of this action step.

Pray to let go of the past, to no longer have it control your present moment, to release yourself from the pain and suffering that is consuming you.

I used to get hung up on how to pray, who to pray to, whether to call it praying! It was a ball of craziness in my head. Now, I don't overthink it. I just send my prayer out there and say, "I have done all I can do. I'm not sure where to go from here. Please take this pain and suffering and show me the way. Give me a sign."

Step 8: Choose Peace Within

Often we are living in a state of reacting. Unhappy, painful past events can bring depression, physical ailments and disturbing behaviour into our lives if we don't process them. It's important for our well-being to learn to let go of the pain and suffering of the past. This is not to say that we ever rid ourselves of it completely, but when the pain and suffering show up, we can plan to consciously process and release it, until it returns.

In this step, we consciously choose peace within. Often, we didn't have a choice about past events, but today, now, we have a choice about how we decide to live.

When we are in the process of letting go of the past—for example, negative feelings as a result of a friend who has hurt us—we have a choice to give up the sweet feeling of revenge. And we have a choice of whether we walk away from situations where we could choose to fight back. Sometimes fighting is the correct response—when it is done from peace within. It is not about gritting your teeth and walking away, or putting on a happy smile while fuming underneath. We can fight a fair fight without anger and resentment.

Our goal is not to deny anger, fear or upset. Choosing peace within means observing our feelings, expressing them when appropriate and then letting them go. It does not mean being a doormat or avoiding confrontation. It means learning how to communicate effectively and act boldly. It is possible to be strong without being aggressive. When choosing peace within, it's okay to be angry; it's not okay to be aggressive. When anger comes up, feel it, process it and then release it.

When you choose peace within, others see that they have a choice too. If we choose to continue to be caught up in our past experiences, pain, suffering, anger, regrets and resentments, we will keep the people around us caught up in them as well. Letting go is the key to family peace and relationship success. It affects the people around you and is an amazing gift to your children, as the ripple effect of your example touches the people in your life. In this step, instead of waiting for others to let go of their past and treat you as you wish, it's up to you to go first. The only person you have control over is yourself.

Action Steps: Choose Peace Within

1. Look at yourself in the mirror, stare into your eyes and say, "I can be at peace with this." Use this affirmation daily for three minutes.

2. Journal
    - List all of the positive things about a situation you regret.
    - List all of the positive qualities of the other person involved.
    - Write down five special times or things that occurred during that period in your life.

* * *

After moving through the eight steps of letting go of the past, you might like to integrate the letting go into your mind, body and energy field. You can use the following meditation to do this.

MEDITATION: LETTING GO OF THE PAST

Close your eyes and relax your body. Sit in an open posture with your feet flat on the floor and your hands facing upwards in your lap.

Take three deep breaths, in through your nose and out through your mouth.

Say: "I release all negative energy, emotions, vibrations and all negative thoughtforms and beliefs from my mind, body and energy field now."

Breathe in and release from everywhere. Do this three times.

Read these words:

May I know that I am fully supported. I am safe. Any emotion that comes up is okay. Let it flow. This is a safe place to be open and honest. I ask to become clear on what I need to let go of in my life in order to create the life and relationships I dream of.

As I focus on letting go of the past may I embody the belief that the past is finished. That it's essential to my happiness that I learn from it and let it go. May I be fully supported in integrating this.

When I move on from the past, more of my gifts and personality emerge.

May I find the courage to understand that I am often holding on to my pain far beyond its ability to serve me because it gives me a sense of identity. I may replay past mistakes over and over again, allowing feelings of shame and regret to shape my actions in the present. My past actions and experiences do not define me. They are what I experienced or did, not who I am.

Let Go of the Past

By letting go I'll experience more happiness and peace. If I let go a little, I will have a little peace. If I let go a lot, I will have a lot of peace.

I'm learning to let go of the past, in particular of all the attitudes, emotions, beliefs, fears, regrets, hurt, sadness and baggage that are holding me back. This is one of the keys to my happiness and allows me to heal my present life. It's a must to make room for more wonderful things to come into my present life.

Letting go of the past not only helps me live my best life now but also paves the way for future success in my life.

If I am haunted by my past and can't move on from it, then it will affect my present and my future.

Now, think now of the past experience, regret, situation that you'd like to let go of. See it, feel it, bring it into your mind.

Read out loud:

I now know the process of how to let go and release myself from this past event. I know that this will be hard and emotional at times. During these times, I'll remember that I am fully supported in this process. The intention of this process is to bring healing, joy, love and peace into my life, and I am ready to begin.

Take three deep breaths in through your nose and out through your mouth.

Bring your awareness back into your body.

* * *

Letting go of the past is an ongoing process that involves feeling some initial pain. It's not easy, and it won't happen overnight. It requires loads of compassion for ourselves and for those around us. But it is worth it. Letting go of the past is the key to our growth and development throughout this life. In time, we can learn to let the negative thoughts feelings from past events go and live in the present moment free from old pain and suffering.

This makes me think of the way Elizabeth Gilbert describes how she handles fear in her book *Big Magic*. She says, "I recognize and respect that you are part of the family, and so I will never exclude you from our activities, but still—your suggestions will never be followed. You're allowed to have a seat, and you're allowed to have a voice, but you are not allowed to have a vote. You're not allowed to touch the road maps; you're not allowed to suggest detours; you're not allowed to fiddle with the temperature. Dude, you're not even allowed to touch the radio. But above all else, my dear old familiar friend, you are absolutely forbidden to drive."

This is precisely what this process of letting go of the past is all about. Not banishing the past experiences, pain and suffering from our lives but rather arriving at a place where we recognize and respect that the pain and suffering of the past are part of the family, but they are forbidden to drive any longer.

Wow! You are in the home stretch of erecting the pillars of a strong, connected and fulfilling relationship. The final pillar that creates a strong, stable foundation is for you and your beloved to get on the same team.

PILLAR 8

Get on the Same Team

"When ego says, 'What am I not getting?' in a relationship, Spirit says, 'What am I not giving?'"
—MARIANNE WILLIAMSON

I remember driving down my driveway away from my house with my phone cutting in and out as I said to my BFF, "I can't do this. I can't continue in a relationship where I feel so alone. I think I need to leave." I breathed and I cried and I stopped my car. I hung up and asked myself, or whoever might be listening, "Why do you feel alone?" The answer I heard was, "Because you have one foot out the door. You are in this with your baby toe. You are constantly saying, 'This isn't going to work.' You are constantly telling Jaye, 'I'm just not happy. I feel alone. I don't know if this is going to work.' If you want a thriving relationship and you want to feel connected and like you aren't alone, you must be here. One hundred percent. You must decide that you are in this, for now at the very least."

So, with this guidance, I turned my car around and then walked back into our home. I sat with Jaye and told him all I had realized. And I said, "I am here. I am fully committed. I want this to work and I am prepared to give it my all. I believe that we can create the thriving marriage we both desire, and I'd like to do that with you, together."

He smiled and let out a sigh of great relief and said, "I've been waiting for you. Let's do this."

The energy of our relationship changed immediately. It went from one where we felt like we were against each other, keeping score and constantly letting each other down. To one where we were on the same team, united in creating the relationship we both desired. We were committed, and we were consciously making our choices.

There is a perfect storm that occurs in some relationships where the pain and suffering become unbearable and the storm is going to either drown the relationship or make you stronger, more experienced sailors. Jaye and I were lucky enough to have it happen for us. During our relationship, we have hit some hard times. There were times when I was 100 percent willing and ready to get in fully and give it my all. These times usually did not coincide with when Jaye was 100 percent willing and ready to get in fully and give it his all. So we were like an elastic being pulled from both ends. The tension of the elastic became so tight that at any moment any little thing could make it bust and snap our fingers. Finally, we hit the perfect storm where we were both 100 percent willing and ready to get in fully and give it our all. This timing made all the difference. The powerful force of this timing allowed us to say, "We aren't on opposite teams here. We aren't opponents in a me-against-you game. We are on the same team."

When we are on the same team, we begin to align against the problem instead of against each other. In this unified atmosphere, we have each other's back and there is a strong friendship. This team mentality is a strong predictor that the relationship will thrive and flourish.

What does being on the same team look like?

- You trust each other fully and completely.
- You see yourselves as allies.
- You feel that you have each other on your side.
- You know that you will conquer problems together.
- You feel safe and secure in your relationship.
- You honour, respect and accept each other.
- You can communicate about conflict in a kind and effective way.
- You regularly connect physically, emotionally and intimately.
- You have lots of joy, fun and peace.
- You support each other's hopes and dreams.
- You are each other's cheerleaders and biggest supporters
- You share important decisions.

It's nearly impossible to create a thriving relationship if the two parties are on opposite teams. So the final pillar of a strong, connected and fulfilling relationship is to get on the same team by following these seven steps:

1. Decide
2. Repair Damage
3. Communicate
4. Set Boundaries
5. Ditch Control
6. Unclench & Have Faith
7. Change Your Relationship Mindset

Step 1: Decide

There are the regular everyday disagreements that occur in a relationship, and then there are the big, devastating, everything-changes-in-an-instant moments. In these moments, trust can be destroyed by one bad decision. In these instances, we find ourselves at a crossroads where we must decide which path to take.

When hard things happen in our relationships, like infidelity, lies, loss, etc., especially if they sideswipe us and we feel like they have come out of nowhere, we can handle these situations in a way that we never dreamed we would.

I have a friend who was sure that she knew exactly what she would do should such a circumstance occur in her marriage. She would pack her bags, or more likely she would throw his shit on the front lawn and kick him out. She was sure she would hate him if this moment came and never be able to forgive him, and the marriage would be over—no questions asked. When we go through devastating, mistake-filled phases of our relationships, we can have a very stringent, no-room-for-mistakes attitude where there is no room for movement.

Yet when she was faced with the reality of this kind of situation, this wasn't her response at all. She found herself ripped wide open and feeling compassion and understanding for her beloved, and love and support for the mistake he had made. She realized things had to have been so bad, that he was hurting so bad, for him to make a bad decision. A mistake he couldn't take back. In the days that followed, she realized he had been hurting as badly in their relationship as her. That the relationship had deteriorated to a point where they were both in turmoil. The relationship had finally hit its rock bottom, where there was no way to go but up. The mistake became the opportunity for them to begin to rebuild their relationship. To heal. There was no longer the option to continue to pretend or ignore the problem. It was right in their face.

My friend told me that when she watched other women stay in their relationship in similar situations she saw courage. She thought they were brave and it inspired her that they would take the chance and work to build a better marriage. She decided to view the rock bottom of her marriage as a place to build from.

However, I have another dear friend who hit rock bottom in her marriage and decided to emerge from the rubble of the broken foundation, leave and save herself. She too has unbelievable courage and bravery. To be able to face the terrible words and judgment of others, their lack of understanding, and stand in her truth. To be, as she puts it, at peace. This takes courage.

The reality of a long-term relationship is we will come to a crossroads where we need to either decide to repair the damage or decide that the damage is too extensive to be repaired. Like each of the eight pillars of relationship revival, the choice is yours.

ACTION STEP: DECIDE

1. Make a Choice
When huge events happen in our relationships, we have a choice. One, to decide it's the final straw and end the relationship. Or two, to decide that it's an opportunity to begin to rebuild the foundation of the relationship from the ground up. It can be the brick wall that forces us to stop and pay attention that we talked about in the second pillar. Looking back, we will see many small things (the pebbles that were being thrown at us) that were quietly whispering, "Hey, look over here. Something isn't right. Something needs to change." If we decided to ignore those things, then when we look back, we'll see that larger things started to occur (the rocks that were being thrown at us) that were yelling at us and becoming harder and harder to ignore. And if we still decided to ignore these rocks being thrown at us, then when we look back, we'll see where the brick wall started to be built up. The enormous things that scream at us so loud and are impossible to ignore. When we hit this brick wall, we know there is no more ignoring. No more pretending. Now we are faced with the consequences of our ignoring and pretending. Now we must deal.

This is the moment when we are ripped wide open. It's the moment when we can't ignore or pretend any longer. It's the moment when we feel like the rug has been ripped out from under us. It's the moment when, quite literally, our knees give out and we hit the floor.

If we choose to stay and repair the damage, that opening becomes the place where we have no choice but to be vulnerable. Vulnerability is the key to rebuilding the rubble, the building blocks of our foundation.

To stay or to leave is a choice that each individual who has found themselves in the rubble has to make. Each situation is unique and this decision is complex. Know that if you find yourself in this place, when you take the time to connect with yourself and when you have the courage to follow your truth and guidance, you can't go wrong.

2. Do Everything You Can
If you decide that you are in this and on the same team, it is paramount that you jump in with both feet and do everything you can. Begin with the foundation of the eight pillars in this book. Dig in and dig deep as you both work towards building the relationship that you desire.

3. Lead Where You Are Strong
Often Jaye and I would get into gridlock in our relationship because I would get frustrated with leading the way. This sometimes felt heavy and tiring, like, "I don't want to lead anymore. I don't want to go first." Jaye is capable and strong and always knows what to do. He leads in so many situations. So I turned to him to lead. I turned to him to know what to do, and in the process, I gave away my power to him.

But Jaye tells me that one of my gifts is my emotional intelligence. It took a long time for me to embrace this and fully understand that this ability means I often need to go first. To lead the way because he doesn't have the skills, it doesn't come naturally to him. The things that I see plain as day are confusing to him. I needed to embrace that these were my gifts to share. Then I needed to understand and have compassion for the fact that he may not be able to lead in this situation, and realize that maybe now it was my turn.

If you want to continue to grow and connect in your relationship, then you must continue to step up and use your unique skills, knowledge and innate understanding to lead where you are strong.

STEP 2: REPAIR DAMAGE

Conflict will occur in our relationships, and there is no way around it. We can decide to view conflict as an indication that we need to put the brakes on or as an opportunity to explore the reason the conflict is occurring. If we choose to explore, we allow the conflict to become the catalyst for the change and transformation we seek. In this step, we begin to emerge from the rubble and rebuild the foundation. We are striving for healing that transforms and turns tragedy into triumph, creating something new. The following steps will guide you in the process of repairing damage, both old ruptures and new fractures, and restoring trust.

ACTION STEPS: REPAIR DAMAGE

1. Release & Reset

After we have had an argument with our beloved, we might we feel depressed, angry, resentful or unwell. Our relationship might feel heavy with congested and stuck energy. This can feel like trying to put one foot in front of the other while wearing boots full of cement. Use the following two rituals to clear, purify and neutralize the energy of your relationship, as well as your home:

a. Clear Negative Energy

You can use the smoke from dried herbs to clear negative energy from you, your home and your relationship. The smoke from the herb attaches itself to negative energy as it dissipates. The smoke takes negative energy with it, and then Mother Earth reabsorbs the negative energy and filters it.

Use this ritual to reset the energy of your relationship once you've decided to get on the same team, and continue to use it periodically throughout the year when major damage occurs or you can feel the energy getting heavy in your life and relationship.

You can do this ritual on your own or with your beloved. I encourage you to ask your beloved for permission before clearing your shared space, as you both live there. However, like all the techniques I share in this book, this ritual is useful and powerful even if only one partner participates.

What you'll need:
- Dried sage bundle (make your own or buy from a metaphysical store): burn to clear negative energy
- Crystals: wear to absorb negative energy so that it doesn't get absorbed by your energy body
- Feather/hand: wave to direct the smoke
- Open windows: to allow the smoke to exit, taking negative energy with it

Light the sage bundle and let it catch fire. Then extinguish the fire in a small bowl but leave the ends smouldering and let the smoke billow from the sage bundle. Allow the smoke to flow freely and make sure to catch the ashes in the bowl.

Begin with clearing and purifying yourself and your beloved, if they are participating. Begin at your feet and work your way up to your head with the smoke, then back down again. You can use a feather or your hand to direct the smoke.

As you do this, visualize the smoke taking away any negative energy, any darkness from your life.

Say: "Air, fire, water, earth. Cleanse, dismiss, dispel."

Now, move on to your space (your house). Walk around your

home, letting the smoke flow everywhere. Go into each room and open all the cupboards and closet doors. Wave smoke into all the corners, across all doorways and into all shadowy spaces.

Use one of the following prayers as you move throughout the house. Say it over and over again. Choose the one that resonates most with you. Or move between several of them.

- "Into this smoke, I release all energies that do not serve me, all negativity that surrounds me and all fears that limit me. So it is."
- "Smoke of air and fire of earth. Cleanse and bless this home. Drive away all harm and fear; only good may enter here."
- "I rid any negative energies and only allow love and joy to flood our space. May the blessings from above shower this space."
- "I release all energies that are no longer in service to my greatest good. I ask that only love, light, health, wealth, happiness and abundance fill my space. And so it is."

When you enter your bedroom, the sacred place where you and your beloved come together, take special care to add specifics about your relationship.

Say, "I release all energies of anger, frustration, hurt, pain and suffering (add your own specifics here for the damage that is occurring in your relationship), and I invite in all energies of love, acceptance, respect, and honouring each other (add your own specifics here of what you want more of in your relationship) to fill our space."

Once you have completed your house and bedroom, extinguish the sage bundle and leave the windows open for a bit to allow the smoke to carry the negative energy out of your space.

b. Release Energy

When we live together and share so much of ourselves with each other—energetically, physically, emotionally and spiritually—naturally, there is a build-up of negative energy and emotions. And when damage has occurred in our relationships, we will be left holding a great deal of each other's energy and emotions.

Use this practice as a catch-all for releasing energy and emotions that you have taken on from your beloved. Also, use this practice to reset the energy of your relationship, and then use it regularly as maintenance. Do this daily to ensure you are releasing energy and emotions that are not yours.

You can also use this practice when you feel yourself being drained by what your beloved has going on in their life. Jaye lives a high-paced, stressful life where he is under tons of pressure daily. I am here as support for him to lean on, yet sometimes I feel drained by it all. When I find myself in this state, I quickly do the following steps and it helps me release the negative energy and emotions:

- Close your eyes and say, "I now isolate and release all negative energy, negative emotions, negative vibrations, negative thought forms and beliefs that are not mine and that are not for my highest good from my mind, my body and my energy field now."
- Breathe in and release from everywhere.
- Repeat three times.

2. Build Trust

After we have made the decision to stay and repair our relationship, and we have released and reset the negative energy, it is essential to rebuild the trust that has been broken. To begin, follow these steps:

a. Ask for & Tell the Truth

Request and give the facts, the truth (not all the gory details, but the truth), and know that living in reality is always better than living in an illusion, though it may not feel like it at the time.

I have been through many circumstances where knowing the truth felt much better than being lied to and then finding out the truth later. When we make a mistake and then lie about it, the damage of the mistake is compounded by the lying.

Often, people will withhold the truth because they're trying to protect or avoid hurting the other person. Whether we tell the truth or hide it, the energy of the truth still seeps into our relationships. The truth will come out eventually, or it will eat us alive from the inside out.

b. Be Accountable

Own your part. If you messed up, admit it. Be accountable for your actions. Even if you didn't realize that you were messing up at the time, once you realize you did, be accountable for it.

If you are the one who is dealing with your beloved's mistakes, you must also own your part. Dig into what feelings are real now and what are old wounds from the past that have been ripped open by the event. In many cases, it is the collision of our past experience with the current circumstances that causes the devastation.

Be accountable for your part. This will help you and your beloved gain mutual understanding of each other's perspective in the situation.

3. Apologize

Once you have heard and told the truth, and owned your part, it's time to begin to mend what was broken. Sometimes that is trust, respect, feelings, etc. The starting point for healing is to apologize for what you are accountable for.

Often, Jaye doesn't fully understand why I am so devastated. To him, from his perspective, it's no big deal. To me, with my life experiences and scars, it is a huge deal. What makes all the difference is Jaye's ability to say, "I messed up and now I need to rebuild what I have destroyed with my mistake."

The apology doesn't take away what was done, but it makes a path to move forward.

4. Offer Forgiveness

We need to do a great deal of forgiveness of our beloved and ourselves as we navigate our relationship and get on the same page. Forgiveness is the foundation of moving forward. It's also incredibly hard to do when we feel deeply hurt and betrayed.

The beginning of the forgiveness process starts with the intention to see the other person as a human being. Again, it's not making excuses for their actions, but it's gaining understanding and having compassion for the other person's humanity.

5. Continue to Repair

When a devastating situation occurs and you have taken the first four steps in the process of repairing damage, be prepared that that is not the end of the process. When scars have been ripped open and new wounds formed, it takes time to heal and move on. To continue to rebuild, it's necessary to do ongoing repair of each little bit of damage that occurs in your relationship. Keep working the steps of Pillar 7 to move on from the damage of past events and quickly repair any new damage that occurs.

While repairing damage and building trust to get on the same team, communication will be key.

STEP 3: COMMUNICATE

When you and your beloved are getting on the same team, it's imperative to keep the lines of communication open. To do this, use the techniques in Pillar 4, and try the following technique of the circle of communication to stay on the same team.

Action Steps: Communicate

The circle of communication creates a safe place for each person to share their truth. Follow these steps to guide you through the circle of communication ritual.

1. Set the Stage

To begin the ritual, choose a centrepiece that represents your willingness to participate in the circle and honour the circle's ways. This could be your wedding rings or something that represents your relationship or something that is important to each of you.

Then choose a talking piece. This talking piece indicates whose turn it is to talk. What happens in regular communication, especially when there are heightened emotions, is that when one person is talking and sharing their truth the other person is waiting in response mode. The talking piece signals us to listen fully and completely. It allows us to follow the old saying that Jaye's grandpa taught us: "You have two ears and one mouth. You should be using your ears twice as much as your mouth."

Our talking piece is a rock we found on the beach of our favourite family vacation spot. If I am holding the rock, it is my turn to talk. And when it's my turn to talk, Jaye's only job is to listen.

2. Begin

Pass the talking piece back and forth, giving each person the space to share their truth.

In difficult times of conflict, you can ask specific questions and each person has a turn to answer them.

For example:
- "How do you feel about the situation that occurred?"

- "How do you think we should handle it?"
- "What do you need?"

Follow these guidelines through the process:
- The person who is holding the talking piece is the only one who talks.
- The other person's only job is to listen.
- This is not a conversation. There is no back and forth. This is a platform for each person to share their truth and then hear the other person's truth.
- This process allows for understanding and space to be held for each participant.

Step 4: Set Boundaries

Navigating the natural give and take in relationships can be difficult. Being on the same team means that we acknowledge that our beloved will inevitably have different perspectives than us, which will lead to us each learning where our boundaries are and how to set clear boundaries to avoid turmoil.

A boundary is essentially a method of drawing a line in the sand. I like to imagine it like a fence, something that keeps you in and others out, a marker of the place where "appropriate" and "inappropriate" meet each other. The place where what you are okay with and what you are not okay with are communicated. A boundary is saying, "I can accept that you may be late coming home from work, yet I would like the courtesy of a phone call letting me know that you won't be making it home to eat with us." Boundaries are essential to healthy relationships.

If we have wishy-washy boundaries—or no boundaries!—we might feel like our agenda is being hijacked all the time, like we're just along for the ride, being pulled this way and that. We'll begin to feel like we are living a life that someone else wants us to live instead of the one we want. We can lose sight of who we are and what our life is about because we aren't taking the time to understand what our boundaries are and then set them in a loving and effective way. Setting boundaries with our beloved is a delicate art, one that needs to be mastered if we are going to have long-term happiness in our intimate relationship.

To set and communicate our boundaries, we must first understand what our boundaries are. We can begin to figure this out by paying attention to when we are triggered. We all have our triggers, those bits of us that have been formed by past experiences. We are triggered when these areas get rubbed by something someone says or does and we feel an emotion arise. The temptation is to say that it is the other person's fault, and if they would just stop doing and saying things that trigger us, then we would feel better. But our power lies in knowing the truth that being accountable for our triggers means understanding that our upset always says more about us and our "unfinished business" being projected onto the current situation or person than it does about them.

Being triggered and the resulting conflict that can arise are a window into our wounds that have yet to be healed and where our boundaries are. Using our triggers as a sign that this is an area we can work to heal and set a boundary leaves us feeling more empowered, helps us understand ourselves better and ultimately expands our capacity for deeper love for ourselves and our beloved.

Action Steps: Set Boundaries

1. Identify Your Boundaries

The first step to setting a boundary is to first identify what your boundary in the situation is. Take time to understand yourself and what you are okay with and what you aren't okay with. Boundaries are tricky. Often we are unaware that the reason we are feeling upset, controlled or uncomfortable is because a boundary, that we are not always conscious of, is being crossed. This first step is extremely important because without knowing what our boundaries are we will not be able to effectively communicate and set the boundary with our beloved.

Ask yourself:
In what situations in my relationship do I feel like I need stronger boundaries?

The first clue that we have a boundary that has been crossed is when we feel triggered—that uncomfortable, controlled, hijacked feeling. To figure out what boundary we need to set, we must first take time to do the inner reflection to get clear within ourselves.

The most effective way to begin this process of identifying your boundaries is to tune in to your feelings.

a. Tune In to Your Feelings
You can use many different techniques in this step: journalling, breathing, talking it out with an uninvolved third party, meditating and so on.

Allow yourself to really feel the emotions that arise. You want to get below your secondary, reactive feelings and thoughts—anger, blame—to the primary, vulnerable feelings of disregarded, disconnected, hurt, helpless, insecure. Make sure you don't mistake thoughts for feeling.

Ask yourself:
- Where am I feeling trampled on, disrespected, hijacked or controlled?

Choose one of the situations you identified and ask yourself:
- What are my boundaries?
- How can I actively set and maintain these boundaries?

b. Practice Self-Awareness

The practice of identifying boundaries has us diving headfirst into more self-awareness. It's difficult to understand our boundaries if we are living unconsciously, so we must take the time to become more self-aware.

This self-awareness looks like paying attention. When you feel uncomfortable, angry, upset, controlled, etc., say to yourself, "Interesting. I acknowledge that this feeling is coming up." Then check in and contemplate, "What is this feeling about. What boundary have I not set that needs to be set?"

This step of self-awareness is all about gaining greater understanding of yourself and your boundaries.

c. Use the Past to Understand the Present

When identifying your boundaries it can be helpful to look at how past events, situations and circumstances are effecting your present. This will give you deeper understanding of why you have these specific boundaries.

We are deeply influenced by the patterns we observed and learned about very early in life, which now live inside us.

Ask yourself:
- When have I felt this feeling before in my life?
- What past event, situation or circumstance is affecting this present situation?
- What is real now?

When big things happen in relationships it will often trigger old pain. Scars from the past will be ripped open, and this can cause great confusion. Past and present can become muddled together and very difficult to navigate.

Asking yourself what is real now so that you can differentiate between what is past pain resurfacing and what is happening now.

- What boundary needs to be set today, and what needs to be let go off from the past?

d. Seek Support

Identifying your boundaries can be confusing and difficult, so support from an uninvolved third party can be very beneficial. Ensure that the person you turn to for support has the skills to not triangulate or pour fuel on the fire. You want to find a person who can hold space for you as you go through your process. This can be a friend, a family member, a counsellor, a spiritual mentor, etc.

I like to seek support from different people at different times. And I usually ask for guidance on how best to deal with what's occurring for me. Sometimes that guidance will be to journal and work through it on my own. Other times it will be to call my soul sister who has known me since I was a kid. She knows my past and what makes me tick. She is able to help me see things that I am unaware of. And still other times I reach out for an energy healing from my spiritual mentor.

Seek out your support when you need it. Reach out and allow yourself to receive the support. You don't have to do this alone.

2. Set Your Boundaries

a. Give Yourself Permission

Once you have identified your boundaries, give yourself permission to set those boundaries. Know that by setting boundaries, you are taking care of yourself and setting your relationship with your beloved up for success. When we ignore our boundaries for various reasons, from not wanting to rock the boat to not realizing we have a boundary that needs to be addressed, we inadvertently set ourselves up to face a crossed boundary and the conflict and emotions that can trigger. We will have to deal with the consequences one way or another.

Give yourself permission to honour and value yourself and your boundaries. Give yourself the freedom to explore what you are okay with and what you aren't, what you can and can't tolerate. Allow this area of boundary-setting to be a place where you get to know yourself on a deeper level, where you say, "This is who I am and what I am okay with and this is where my boundaries are." Give yourself permission for your boundaries to be okay—embrace them, even when setting them is difficult.

If we have been living with few boundaries, beginning to set them will change the dynamics of our relationship. Your beloved may feel a little off balance for a while as they begin to navigate this new territory with you. As always, be gentle with yourself and your beloved as you practice this art of setting your boundaries.

b. Start Small

If we haven't been setting boundaries regularly, beginning can feel really uncomfortable. As with everything, take the first baby step. Start small and grow into the art of setting your boundaries.

Choose one area you identified above that you haven't set a boundary in and have a discussion with your beloved about it.

One of the first boundaries I discovered was simply about dishes. I felt taken advantage of when Jaye would leave his dishes in the sink instead of loading them in the dishwasher.

c. Be Clear & Direct

In the identifying steps you will have gained greater understanding of yourself, of what your boundaries are and of why you have them. When communicating your boundaries to your beloved, be clear and direct.

For example, about the dishes I said to Jaye, "I feel frustrated when the dishes are left in the sink instead of being loaded into the dishwasher. I wonder if we can come to an agreement that we are each responsible for loading our own dishes into the dishwasher."

This clearly states what is not working and what could be a solution. Jaye then had the opportunity to respond—to agree to my proposed solution or to offer a different solution and/or more information.

d. Gain Understanding

In the dishes situation, Jaye offered more information about why he leaves his dishes in the sink instead of loading them. It had to do with the difference in how we were raised. In his house growing up, he was to leave his dishes in the sink, as his mom liked to load the dishwasher in a certain way. Whereas I was always expected to load my own dishes. So when he wasn't loading his in our home I felt like he was taking advantage of me and treating me like his maid.

This added information allowed me to gain more understanding of Jaye's perspective. This new understanding allowed me to see where he was coming from, and my explanation allowed him to see where I was coming from. This brief conversation cleared up so many assumptions I was making. In the end, we agreed on what our home's dishes etiquette would be and the boundary was set.

e. Reset When Needed

Once a boundary has been set, each time it is crossed, it needs to be reset. This is a training process, for ourselves and our beloved. If we have been doing things one way for a time and now we are saying, "This is my boundary," it will take time to condition ourselves to this change.

Resetting the boundary can be a gentle reminder. In the dishes example, when Jaye forgets to load his dishes, I gently say, "Can you please load your plate and wine glass?"

* * *

Boundaries are essential to healthy relationships and, really, a healthy life. Identifying, setting and sustaining boundaries are skills. Like any skills the more we do them the more we master them.

STEP 5: DITCH CONTROL

Being on the same team requires us to understand that two lives don't become one in the sense that you must agree and do everything on the same path. We still remain individuals with free will, even when we're in an intimate relationship.

If we feel our beloved pulling away we'll start to feel insecure and find ourselves trying to control everything. This creates an atmosphere of co-dependency and control, which leads to feelings of suffocation and powerlessness. The more one person tries to control the other, often under the guise of "This is how a relationship should work. We are a partnership, so we need to agree and decide on everything you do in your life," the harder the other person will pull to "break free" and do things in response like not communicating what they are doing because they do not want to be berated.

When we love and live our truth and honour that in our beloved, we create an interdependent relationship where we build a life together yet have our own separate lives as well. This is how we create a relationship where we love in a way that the other person feels free.

ACTION STEPS: DITCH CONTROL

1. Identify Unmet Expectations

Pain and suffering occur when we have expectations of our beloved that aren't met.

I was reminded of this lesson during the heart-wrenching and extremely difficult time of having to put our twelve-year-old bull mastiff, Kaido, down. When things like this happen, what I need and what Jaye needs are not always the same. Actually, scratch that—they are rarely the same. And when I hold on to preconceived expectations of what I expect him to do that go unmet, and vice versa, we both experience additional pain and suffering.

In this example of having to say goodbye to our family pet, my pain was compounded by the desire and expectation that Jaye be there with me, but this situation didn't easily allow for that.

Kaido hadn't been well for a few weeks, but he seemed to be on the upswing. Jaye had a business trip planned, and the night before he left, Kaido ended up having surgery. After surgery, the vet called and said he was doing quite well; however, he wasn't breathing as well as she'd like. She wanted to keep him overnight. But she felt he was stable and would make a full recovery.

The next morning, Jaye got up to drive to his business appointment in the neighbouring town. I got up and got the kids off to school. When the vet's office opened, she gave me a call and told me Kaido still wasn't breathing well. She suggested I come for a visit. I spent most of the day there.

Jaye and I were in constant contact about how Kaido was doing. But by the end of the day, Kaido took a turn for the worse, and he was in great pain and unable to breathe well. He kept looking at me and using his paw to pat me, saying, "Mom, it's okay. It's time."

2. Let Go
We have the power to let go of our attachment to the expectations we have of each other and instead decide to say, "I'll do me and you do you."

In major life situations, I have the desire to be there through it all, and I know that Jaye doesn't have the same need to be needed and give support until the very end. This is a pattern in my life.

At times throughout the day with Kaido, I felt upset and unsupported and alone. Fortunately, I bumped into a friend while grabbing a coffee—thank you, universe!—who kindly offered me the perspective that in times like this it is essential to allow each person to do as they need. To honour each other through the process. She said, "You do you and let him do him."

Embracing this new perspective changed my entire experience. It allowed me to let go of this upset that Jaye wasn't there with me in the way I expected. This new perspective challenged me to decide whether I wanted to experience this day from a place of hurt, anger and frustration or from a place of honouring that I was doing me—being there, nurturing Kaido—and Jaye was doing what he needed to do. It reminded me that that is okay. It allowed me to do what I needed and to feel grateful that I was able to be there with Kaido on his last day. Once I decided to let go of my expectations, the pain and suffering went away, and I was able to authentically experience my own process and let Jaye have his without the weight of my unmet expectations.

3. Seek Support

This experience also reminded me of the lesson I had learned long ago but seem to need reminding of over and over again. Our beloved cannot be our everything. In some situations, our primary source of support will not come from our beloved—and this is okay. This is why we have friends and family and colleagues. We are surrounded by love and support from others—all we have to do is reach out and receive that support when we need it. It's hard for me to let people in, to admit I need them.

But my soul sister was sent to me that day to remind me of this and to show me that even when I don't know what I need, or am too scared to ask, they are there carrying me when I'm unable to do it myself. After I got the call from the vet to visit Kaido, my friend Jenn said she'd come with me. I found myself telling her she didn't have to come. I felt embarrassed by my unmet expectations of my husband that I was grappling with and felt I should be able to handle things myself. But when I was visiting Kaido in the back room at the vet's, my phone dinged with a text from Jenn: "I'm here in the lobby if you need me. If not, I'll just be here if you decide you do."

I did, and she sat with Kaido and me for an hour, holding my hand. I was quietly reminded that I am not in this life alone. I am in this life only with Jaye. I am also surrounded by my friends and family. It's my job to call upon them and open myself to receiving their help and support. Expecting our beloved to fulfill all these roles for us puts too much pressure on the relationship. Building and using our sisterhood allows our needs to be met outside of our relationship.

I found my support in my friend that day, and later I thanked her for being there with me. For knowing what I needed better than I did and for following her intuition and reaching out, even though I was pushing her away. I said, "I struggle asking for help. I struggle knowing when I need support. I struggle not being able to handle everything myself and admitting this." I know that I depend greatly on Jaye to fulfill much of this needed support for me. And I know that this puts a great deal of pressure on our relationship, especially when he is unable to meet those needs and expectations. My friend and I vowed that night to support each other when needed. I felt a huge relief and felt less alone. And I could let go a little more of this old, deep-seated belief that our beloved is meant to be our everything and our only.

Our human needs are complex and varied. It is way too much pressure and completely unrealistic to expect that one human being could be our everything—or even our mostly. Find support for both big emotional events and the everyday duties of life in your community. Lean on your friends and family and allow them to support you. Remember that you don't have to do everything alone. Open yourself up to receiving support.

* * *

In times when you realize you have unmet expectations of how your beloved should show up, take a second to breathe and let go of control. Remember, you are each individuals and you need to honour each other's process.

Step 6: Unclench & Have Faith

I am a huge believer in being the captain of our own ship. In both our life and in our relationship. Yet although we're the captain, there's something much bigger than us out there steering the ship.

Using the tools, strategies and techniques I have shared throughout this book, we can gain control in many areas, including what thoughts and beliefs we decide to let take up residence in our minds. But sometimes when we are talking about relationships, especially if we are trying to move on from old hurt, pain and suffering, we might say, "I'm trying everything. I'm doing the work. I'm doing the connection work. I'm doing the communication work. I'm being consistent. I'm following through, but I'm still not seeing the results I want."

Now is the time to say, "Okay, I have done all I can. now it's time to unclench and let go of expectations and attachments and allow the things that I couldn't have thought of, or have not yet come to see, to unfold before me." In this unclenching we must find a way to have faith that our plan may not turn out as we had hoped. But that a greater plan is unfolding.

The amazing—and hard—thing is that our "plan" is sometimes not working out because there is a greater plan for us. We just can't see what or why yet. The tricky part is to embrace the unplanned and find a way to integrate this idea that everything is happening as it should and the reasons as to why are not yet known.

It's time to unclench when we find ourselves holding on too tight to our vision, our plan or our steps to implement the plan. When we find ourselves in tunnel vision, we can begin to feel defeated. In these times, remember that you are not defeated. You did not fail. You need to pivot. It is time to flex the muscle of flow.

We need to stop crowding the energy space with fear and worry. Release the worry, the fear, the expectations and the attachment. When we release the need to control the how, if and when, we allow room for it all to flow in.

Unclench, dear friend. It's holding you back. Breathe and ask for assistance, guidance, support and signs. Accept that you aren't in control of everything. You can't be. Plan. Do. Believe. And then lean back, unclench, release and let it all go. Make space for it all to flow.

Action Step: Unclench & Have Faith

When you are feeling totally defeated, when you feel like wave after wave is hitting you and you can't to catch your breath, it's a sign that it's time to get out of the water, even for just a few minutes every day. Let yourself turn off the pressures, the expectations, the disappointment, the hurt, pain and frustrations. Take a few minutes every day to remember all that you've achieved and how far you've come. Remember all that you love about your beloved. Take a walk down memory lane and recall all those amazing times and let your mind rest from the waves that are hitting you now.

Take time to think of all the moments in your life and in your relationship when you had a plan and that plan didn't pan out, yet a greater plan than you could ever have imagined emerged. Garth Brooks sums it up: "Some of God's greatest gifts are unanswered prayers." Think of all those times that you had unanswered prayers that turned into great gifts.

Step 7: Change Your Relationship Mindset

The last step in the pillar of getting on the same team is to change your relationship mindset. Sometimes we find ourselves taking what we have for granted. This can contribute to a downward spiral. One way to really shake things up in your relationship is to make some radical changes to your mindset.

Action Step: Change Your Relationship Mindset

To change perspective and bring things into focus, try showing up in your relationship as if you or your beloved could be gone tomorrow.

Live from a place with these questions at the top of your mind: "If I only had one more day with my beloved how would I behave? How would I show up? How would I act?"

Ask yourself:
- Would I choose to interact with my beloved like this?
- Would I act like this?
- Would I choose to spend my time like this?
- Would this thing I am upset about still matter?

* * *

Getting on the same team with your beloved will help you create the foundation for a strong, connected and fulfilling relationship. First, you must decide that you are committed to being teammates. That you are ready to say, "I am in, 110 percent. I am ready and willing to turn towards my beloved instead of away from them. I am ready to rebuild the foundation of our relationship by repairing the damage that has occurred, and I am willing to communicate, set boundaries and release the expectations I'm holding on to." Deciding to be teammates instead of opponents will change the way you experience your relationship. You will no longer be turning against each other, instead you will be untied against the problems and working together to build a strong foundation for the relationship you desire.

CONCLUSION

Relationships aren't a fairy tale like the Disney movies depict. Instead, like the black and white sand that Jaye and I combined on our wedding day, they are constantly changing, made of two unique individuals who are coming together as partners in life. No matter how we look at it, that endeavour is a challenge. If we want to experience thriving relationships, we have to consciously construct a strong, stable foundation to build upon. Every time the foundation gets a crack, whether a small fissure or a large chasm, we must work quickly and proactively to repair it. And along the way, it's essential to nurture our relationship through regular communication and connection.

As you moved through the eight pillars of relationship revival in this book, you engaged in a great deal of self-reflection. The first step was to make a choice. To decide if you are in your relationship or if you are not. Staying in limbo causes pain. There is no right or wrong answer. The choice is yours and yours alone. Follow your truth and find peace in making a choice either way.

If you your inner wisdom guided you to reviving your relationship, congratulations on stepping into the driver's seat of your life and making a choice. This should be honoured and celebrated. You've taken the initiative to build the foundation of a strong, connected and fulfilling relationship. The eight pillars in this book will reinforce that foundation.

Return to these pillars regularly. They *are* the foundation of your relationship, and they are all as important as each other. If one pillar is cracked or disintegrated into rubble, the other pillars will falter. Work each pillar in your relationship—be proactive, conscious and deliberate in building and maintaining a strong, stable foundation.

Remember to be gentle with yourself and your beloved as you navigate the phases of your relationship. Focus on the pillars of making a choice, cleaning up your side of the street, creating a relationship vision, communicating, connecting emotionally and sexually, letting go of the past and getting on the same team. And in times of turmoil, revisit these pillars to revive your relationship.

Our relationships go through phases—be prepared for that. Allow these eight pillars to be your guide. Pick up this book when you feel at a loss for what to do and open it anywhere. Whatever page you land on, begin there and fortify your relationship's foundation. These pillars are a constant in a strong, connected and fulfilling relationship. Work them regularly and watch as your foundation becomes stronger and stronger.

Wherever you find yourself in your relationship, may you find a way to honour yourself and your beloved in creating the relationship you desire.

EPILOGUE

"Where are you?"

With a little hesitation, I said, "I'm at the coffee shop, writing."

His response: "Wait there. I'm on my way."

I hung up, wondering what he was up to. And I waited.

He walked into the crowded coffee shop with his signature grin painted on his face. As he strutted towards my table my heart skipped a beat. This man I've loved for fourteen years can still make my heart jump and my cheeks flush. In his hand he held a small white gift bag with polka dot tissue paper popping through the top. He set the bag in front of me and softly said, "It arrived. Sorry it's late. They had to custom-make it."

I opened the bag with great anticipation and felt flutters in my stomach. I fumbled as I tried to open the delicate little box. I noticed with confusion that my hands were shaking.

You see, the reaction I was having isn't something that I experience often. In the beginning of our relationship, I felt these sensations every time Jaye entered a room, but at this stage in our relationship, they occur much less frequently. Okay, if I'm being honest, very infrequently.

But inside the perfect little box was a family ring with his and our kids' birthstones. The beautiful gift he so thoughtfully picked out and designed for our ten-year anniversary to represent our love story and all that we have created. Our intimate energy and the charge of our relationship was on full display to everyone in the coffee shop. My heart skipped a beat because it was so full of love and gratitude for him and for all the ups and downs we've been through. My heart overflowed with all that is and all that could have been—my love for this man. We are so blessed.

ACKNOWLEDGEMENTS & GRATITUDE

Writing this book has been a deep heart project. As with anything from the heart, it was an experience of ups and downs. Through every phase of this book, I have been supported by many individuals whom I would like to thank from the very bottom of my heart.

First, Jaye. Without your willingness to authentically share the ins and outs of our relationship with the world, this book would not exist. Thank you for travelling the journey of life with me and always supporting me in the pursuit of my dreams. I love you.

A huge thank-you to Trevor Warren for sharing your expertise in relationships. Your guidance and support were instrumental in the revival of mine and Jaye's relationship, and many of the pillars in this book. From the bottom of my heart, thank you.

To Kate Muker, my friend, mentor and coach, for always supporting me in aligning with my truth, guidance and inner knowing. The topic of this book was not what I initially thought it would be. I was partway through writing another book when the guidance clearly came through to write my first book on relationships. Kate, your encouragement gave me the courage to trust and follow this guidance. Thank you.

Thank you, Shivonne, for being my biggest cheerleader. For avidly reading my first drafts and lending encouragement and support when my belief in myself wavered.

To Jenn, for being there. Always. Reading and implementing and holding space for me as I move through my creative process. Your unwavering support and belief in me allowed me to borrow it when I need a little extra.

To my mom and dad and grandpa and grandpa, thank you for showing me how to love. For giving me an example of what strong, connected and fulfilling relationships can look like.

Mom, thank you for reading my entire manuscript from beginning to end and giving feedback. But, more importantly, for always being there for me through every phase of my life. I love you.

Taya and Landon, thank you for your pride in me and for all the moments you held space for me to write this book. Your sweet little comments like, "Something I love about my mama is she is following her dreams and publishing her first book" keep me motivated and moving forward towards my dreams. My greatest wish for you is that you too will courageously step out and follow each of your dreams. Love you always and forever.

To my editor, Shirarose Wilensky, thank you for taking my first really rough draft and helping me craft it into this final version. Without your expertise and guidance, I would have struggled to complete this book. I am forever grateful.

To Vanessa Ooms, thank you for capturing my vision for the book cover!

To my girlfriends who read parts of the manuscript and supported me with feedback. Thank you— Nicole, Melissa, Jen, Amber,

Acknowledgements & Gratitude

Christina, Shelly, Kate, Judy, Jenn, Shivonne, Julie and Sandi. And last but definitely not least, to each person who supported my Kickstarter campaign for *Relationship Revival: 8 Pillars of a Strong, Connected & Fulfilling Relationship*—your support means the world to me.

www.ingramcontent.com/pod-product-compliance
Lightning Source LLC
Chambersburg PA
CBHW072155100526
44589CB00015B/2237